Claire Macdonald and her husband run Kinloch Lodge Hotel on the Isle of Skye, which is also the family home for them and their four children. Claire is a well-known exponent of Scottish cooking and travels widely, lecturing and demonstrating recipes.

Claire Macdonald

of Macdonald

Sweet Things

CORGI BOOKS

SWEET THINGS
A CORGI BOOK : 0 552 99217 8

Originally published in Great Britain by
Century Publishing Co Ltd

PRINTING HISTORY
Century edition published 1984
Corgi edition published 1986

9 10 8

Illustrations by Rob Stone

This book is set in 11/12 pt Baskerville.

Corgi Books are published by Transworld Publishers Ltd,
61–63 Uxbridge Road, London W5 5SA,
a division of The Random House Group Ltd,
in Australia by Random House Australia (Pty) Ltd,
20 Alfred Street, Milsons Point, Sydney, NSW 2061, Australia,
in New Zealand by Random House New Zealand Ltd,
18 Poland Road, Glenfield, Auckland 10, New Zealand
and in South Africa by Random House (Pty) Ltd,
Endulini, 5a Jubilee Road, Parktown 2193, South Africa.

Printed and bound in Great Britain by
Cox & Wyman Ltd, Reading, Berkshire.

Acknowledgements

There are so many people I want to thank – first, Gog and our children, Alexandra, Isabella, Meriel and Hugo. They are unendingly tolerant, especially when they are forced to try an experiment which isn't quite the success I'd hoped it might be. Thanks, too, to Peter Macpherson and Wendy Stephen who help me at Kinloch. I am also grateful to special friends who go on inspiring and encouraging me, of them firstly my sisters Camilla Westwood and Olivia Milburn, and then Araminta Dallmeyer, Lucinda Baillie, April Strang Steel, Isobel Sydney, Sue Loudon and my cousin Judith Coleridge. Lastly, thank you to Gail Rebuck and Susan Lamb at Century, and to Gill Edden who painstakingly edited this book and *Seasonal Cooking* before it.

I'd like to dedicate this book to my father and mother, who are equally to blame for my sweet tooth.

Contents

Introduction

I can't imagine that I will ever enjoy writing anything as much as I've enjoyed writing this book. It contains the culinary subjects nearest to my heart – all sweet things. Puddings and preserves, cakes and biscuits, chocolates and fudges, ice creams and chewy meringues, they are all here, all the foods that tempt me most.

There doesn't exist a person better qualified to write a book like this, because I am addicted to all things sweet. This failing could well have been the gift of a bad fairy at my christening, but in fact it wasn't; it is an inherited weakness, for which both my father and mother are equally to blame, it being a strong trait on both sides of the family. Indeed, my father is as untrustworthy as our black whippet Florence when left alone with a box of chocolates. I had hoped that I hadn't passed this craving on to any of our four children, but I'm afraid that each of them is tarred with the same brush as me. I feel wholly responsible for this, as Godfrey, my husband, does not really have a sweet tooth (with one or two exceptions, like Bendicks Bitter-mints, which he insists on keeping in the fridge).

I am lucky, because I am able to do what I enjoy most – cooking – practically every day throughout the year. Kinloch Lodge, where we live, is a small, rather remote hotel. It is set in the most beautiful place, at the foot of a mountain and on the edge of a sea loch on the Isle of Skye. This is the ideal existence for someone like me, because my work is really a form of self-indulgence. I am extremely lucky also in sharing the cooking with Peter Macpherson, who has been with me for nearly thirteen years now, and who is really part of our family. Like me, he is possessed of a very sweet tooth, and so we find no end of inspiration when it comes to the pudding course on the menu for our guests.

The food we produce for the hotel is what I can only describe as 'home dinner party' food, and everything we serve we make ourselves, including the marmalade served at breakfast and the hot cross buns at Easter. Living in Skye, we are rather restricted by the seasons, for which I am glad. Even if I could get them, I don't think I would be at all tempted by strawberries in the middle of winter. I make two exceptions here: we freeze and use throughout the winter raspberries and brambles, both of which make the most delicious hot puddings, of which the best are a steamed suet pudding with blackberries and lemon, and a heavenly warm raspberry and lemon pudding. The seasons bring their own inspiration for puddings for our menus. In summer the warm weather makes me think of creamy ices, subtly flavoured water ices, and refreshing mousses and soufflés. Winter makes me think of mincemeat and apple meringue pie, or hot pineapple meringue pudding. Then, I think that hot sauces can transform a summery pudding into one fit for a winter menu, such as the delectable hot fudge sauce, served with vanilla ice cream, or the rich iced orange cream served with hot chocolate sauce.

The home side of our life here at Kinloch is quite separate from the hotel; I spend my life dashing between the two kitchens! Naturally, any left-over puds from the guest dining room tend to be eaten up by Alexandra, Isabella, Meriel and Hugo. But when I am making a pud for the family, it will tend to be the sort of thing we can't put on the menu for our guests, such as Rice Pudding or Queen of Puddings. We also like to have cakes and home-made biscuits in the tin for tea time, with fudge or treacle toffee for special treats. Wendy Stephen, who helps us to live our lives by looking after our children, has a particularly good line in sweet things herself; the chapter on confectionery contains one of her recipes which is a great favourite with us – Chocolate Fudge Squares.

I have a persistent battle with the bathroom scales, and Godfrey has to be patient with my wails of despair when I discover that my weight has shot up alarmingly after a bout of indulgence which I will grandly refer to as research! This is a penalty of loving good food and, above all, sweet food. But I refuse to give up the good things in life and firmly believe that, as in most things, moderation is the answer. I do hope that you who buy and read this book will get as much pleasure out of making the recipes in it and eating the results as I do.

Ices, Sorbets & Frozen Puddings

We have ices on the menu at Kinloch several times each week. We have been making ice creams and sorbets for years, but recently one of my dreams came true and I became the proud owner of a Gelato Chef – a machine which makes the most superbly textured ice cream I have ever eaten. It churns the ice cream or sorbet mixture as it freezes, then you put the resulting ice into the deep freeze until you are ready to serve it. As all the recipes in this chapter were made and devised years before I got my Gelato Chef, it is by no means essential, just very nice to have.

I do like to serve a sauce with ices, it dresses them up and finishes them off. There is a selection to choose from in the chapter on sauces, all of which would enhance an ice!

Vanilla Ice Cream 1

It would be hard to name the pudding that comes top of my father's list of personal favourites, but if I had to, this would be it. He especially likes it if served with Fudge Sauce (page 157). This is one ice cream which is much easier made in the Gelato Chef, as otherwise it needs to be taken out of the deep freeze and beaten at two or three stages during its freezing time, but to me it is proper vanilla ice cream.

Serves 8

¾ pint (425 ml) single cream	4 oz (125 g) caster sugar
1 vanilla pod	½ pint (300 ml) double cream, whipped but not
6 egg yolks	too stiffly

Put the single cream and the vanilla pod together in a heavy saucepan over a gentle heat. Let it heat slowly until the cream is just beginning to form a skin. Meanwhile, beat the egg yolks, gradually adding the caster sugar. Pour a little of the hot cream on to the yolks and sugar, mix well, then pour in the rest of the hot cream. Mix together well and pour back into the saucepan. Put the pan back on to gentle heat and stir continuously until the mixture is thick enough to coat the back of the wooden spoon. Remove from the heat and leave, with the vanilla pod still in it, to get quite cold. Then remove the pod – I wash and leave mine to dry, and use it again.

Fold the cold cream custard into the whipped cream and put into a polythene container to freeze. Remove it from the freezer after 1½ hours or so, scrape the freezing bits down the sides of the container and beat it well. Return it to the freezer then beat it again after a further 1½–2 hours; if you remember, a third beating gives an even better result!

Should you have an ice cream maker, put the ice cream in to freeze and churn for 25 minutes, then scrape it into a polythene container and keep frozen.

Take the container out of the freezer and leave it at room temperature for 30 minutes before serving.

Vanilla Ice Cream 2

This recipe for vanilla ice cream was given to me several years ago by Caroline Fox. I've been making it ever since, and using it as the base for many ice creams of varying flavours. It needs no beating as it freezes. But, a word of warning: if you use vanilla essence to flavour it, try to eat the ice cream within a couple of weeks of making it, because the flavour of vanilla essence goes off after much more than 3 or 4 weeks in the deep freeze.

Serves 6–8

---

4 eggs, separated	*a few drops of vanilla*
4 oz (125 g) icing sugar,	*essence*
sieved	*½ pint (300 ml) double*
	cream

If you make this ice cream mixture up in the following order, you can use the same pair of whisks without washing them up until the end.

First, put the egg whites into a bowl, and whisk them until they are thick, white and fairly stiff – beginning to stand in soft peaks. Then, a teaspoon at a time, whisk in half the sieved icing sugar, whisking until the meringue mixture is stiff. Next, whisk the yolks, gradually adding the other half of the sieved icing sugar and whisking until the mixture is pale and thick. Whisk in the few drops of vanilla essence. Lastly whip the cream until it has roughly the same consistency as the meringue.

Fold the yolks mixture into the cream, then the meringue mixture, folding all together thoroughly. Pour the mixture into a polythene container, cover, and freeze. Take the container out of the deep freeze and leave at room temperature for about 30 minutes before you want to serve it.

Iced Honey & Whisky Creams

This is a real 'Taste of Scotland' recipe, what with the whisky and the honey. It is extremely easy and quick to make. The recipe was given to me by Margaret Clark, in Edinburgh, and the recipe was given to her with brandy as the alcohol content. Whilst browsing through one of John Tovey's books recently I came across the same recipe with the brandy, so I'm sure his was the original source of inspiration. I asked him whether he minded my including it in this book, and in his usual generous way he not only gave me his blessing to use it, but almost made me feel that the idea had been originally my own! Because of the alcohol in this recipe, the cream never freezes rock hard and so doesn't need to be removed from the deep freeze until just before it is to be served.

Serves 8–9

½ pint (300 ml) double
    cream
4 tablespoons whisky
3–4 tablespoons thick honey

4 egg yolks (use the whites
    to make vanilla ice cream
    or meringues)

Whip the cream, gradually adding the whisky, until fairly thick. Warm the honey in a saucepan until hot and runny. Put the yolks into a bowl and, using a hand-held electric whisk, whisk the yolks, gradually pouring on the hot honey. Whisk until the mixture is thick and pale. This mixture and the whipped cream and whisky should have about the same consistency. Fold both together, and divide between 8 large ramekins or 9 smaller ones. Freeze, and when firm on the surface, cover each one with a piece of cling film.

Coffee & Praline Ice Cream

Serves 6–8

---

4 eggs, separated	Praline:
4 oz (125 g) icing sugar, sieved	*2 oz (50 g) granulated or caster sugar*
1 rounded dessertspoon coffee powder (not granules)	*1 oz (25 g) flaked almonds*
½ pint (300 ml) double cream	

Make the praline first. Put the sugar and almonds together in a small, heavy saucepan. Put the pan over a gentle to moderate heat, until the sugar begins to melt. Shake the saucepan as the sugar melts, until all the sugar has dissolved and is turning a deep golden brown I find that if I turn my back even for a second at this stage the sugar burns, and then I have to throw it away and start again, because of the all-pervading bitter taste of burnt sugar.

Grease a small tin, pour the liquid sugar and almonds on to it and leave to set and cool. Then put a piece of cling film over the cold praline on the tin and bash, using a rolling pin, until the pieces are fairly fine – like coarse breadcrumbs. I find praline-bashing rather therapeutic if my feathers are slightly ruffled!!

Store the crushed praline in a screw-topped jar; it keeps for several weeks.

Whisk the egg whites until fairly stiff then, a teaspoon at a time, whisk in half the icing sugar. Whisk the yolks, adding the remaining sieved icing sugar and the coffee powder. Whisk until thick. Whip the cream, but not too stiffly, and fold the yolk and coffee mixture together, then fold the meringue mixture into this, adding the crushed praline at the same time.

Pour the mixture into a polythene container and freeze. Take the container out of the deep freeze and leave at room temperature for about 30 minutes before you want to serve it.

Peach & Toasted Hazelnut Ice Cream

This is a delicious summery ice cream.

Serves 8

---

6 medium-sized peaches (if they are huge, use only 4)
juice of ½ a lemon
2 oz (50 g) hazelnuts, toasted

4 eggs, separated
4 oz (125 g) icing sugar, sieved
½ pint (300 ml) double cream

Bring a saucepan of water to the boil and stick each peach on the end of a fork into the boiling water for a count of five; remove, and the skins will slip off the peaches easily. Cut each peach in half, and remove the stone, then liquidise the peaches with the lemon juice. Rub the hazelnuts in a tea towel to remove their papery skins. Then put them into a bowl and bash them with a rolling pin, but I like the bits of nut to be quite chunky, not too fine.

Whisk the egg whites until fairly stiff, then add half the

sieved icing sugar, a teaspoon at a time, whisking until the meringue mixture is very stiff. Next whisk the yolks, adding the remaining sieved icing sugar, and whisking until the mixture is pale and thick. Whip the cream, but not too stiffly. Fold the yolks mixture, the puréed peaches, hazelnuts and whipped cream together. Then fold the meringue mixture through it all thoroughly. Pour into a polythene container and freeze.

It is not essential to beat this ice cream half-way through freezing, but it does improve the texture. The flavour is as delicious whether you do or don't beat! Remove the ice cream from the deep freeze and leave at room temperature for 30 minutes before serving.

Brown Bread Ice Cream

I repeat this exquisitely flavoured and textured ice cream unashamedly – it is in my first book, *Seasonal Cooking from the Isle of Skye* – because I feel that no chapter on ice creams would be complete without it. The recipe was given to me originally by Jean Lindsay; since she gave it to me I've come across many recipes for brown bread ice creams and none of them are a patch on this one. It is very easy to make, and draws audible cries of glee and surprise from the dining-room at Kinloch when it is on the menu!

Serves 6

---

3 oz (75 g) wholewheat breadcrumbs – we use crumbs made from the bread we make each day at Kinloch

2 oz (50 g) granulated sugar
¾ pint (425 ml) double cream
3 oz (75 g) icing sugar, sieved
½ teaspoon vanilla essence

Toast the breadcrumbs until they are evenly golden brown all over. Put the sugar into a heavy saucepan, add 3 tablespoons water and heat gently until the sugar has dissolved completely. Then boil fast for 2 minutes. Stir the toasted crumbs into the hot syrup and stir until the syrup cools – the crumbs will become sugar encrusted. Any that form a hard lump can be bashed into smaller bits.

Whip the cream with the icing sugar and vanilla essence and stir in the cooled, sugar-crusted crumbs. Pour the mixture into a polythene container and freeze. Remove the ice cream from the deep freeze as you start dinner, and put it in the fridge. Take it out of the fridge and leave at room temperature as you begin to serve the main course.

Iced Blackcurrant & Mint Parfait

The combined flavours of mint (I use applemint) and blackcurrants are most refreshing. I don't liquidise and sieve the blackcurrants and mint – I put them briefly through the food processor, because I like the rather bitty texture.

Serves 8

1 lb (450 g) blackcurrants, fresh or frozen	*detect the minty flavour at all*
2 good handfuls of mint, stripped from its thicker stems ; this sounds a lot but don't be tempted to use only a couple of sprigs, because then you won't	*4 eggs, separated*
	4 oz (125 g) caster sugar
	½ pint (300 ml) double cream, whipped, but not too stiffly

Put the blackcurrants into a saucepan with a lid on, and put the pan over a fairly low heat. Cook gently until the juices run from the currants. When the currants are soft, take the pan off the heat, cool a bit, then work in the blender or food processor together with the mint leaves, but don't work to a fine purée. Leave to get completely cold.

Put the egg yolks into a bowl, and beat (I use a hand-held electric whisk) gradually adding the caster sugar, until the mixture is pale and thick. Stir the currant and mint mixture into this. Then fold the whipped cream into it too.

Lastly, whisk the egg whites until stiff and peaky and, using a metal spoon, fold this quickly and thoroughly through the creamy mixture. Pour into a polythene container and freeze. Remove the container from the deep freeze at the beginning of dinner and leave at room temperature until you are ready to serve.

Kinloch Chocolate Raisin & Brandy Ice Cream

The basic chocolate ice cream in this recipe is the best I know, and it is originally Katie Stewart's. The wicked embellishments (booze and raisins) are Peter's and mine. The longer you can soak the raisins in the brandy (or you can use rum if you prefer) the better.

Serves 6–8

2 oz (50 g) raisins	3 egg yolks
6 tablespoons brandy	½ pint (300 ml) double
2 oz (50 g) caster sugar	cream, whipped but not
6 oz (175 g) plain chocolate	too stiffly

Put the raisins into a small bowl and measure the brandy into them. Cover with cling film and leave for several hours; the raisins will plump up and absorb most of the brandy. The fumes as you remove the cling film will render you helpless for 30 seconds.

Put the caster sugar and 4 tablespoons water into a small saucepan and place over a gentle heat until the sugar has completely dissolved. Then boil fast for 2–3 minutes. Break the chocolate into a liquidiser or food processor, pour the hot syrup straight from the heat on to the chocolate and whizz to a thick purée. (This makes a dreadful noise initially, but the heat of the syrup very soon melts the chocolate.) Then add the egg yolks, one at a time, blending as you do so. Leave to cool.

When cool, fold together the whipped cream and the rich chocolatey mixture. Lastly fold in the brandy and raisins. Pour the mixture into a polythene container and freeze. This needs no beating during freezing, and it is possible to spoon it straight from the deep freeze but it is easier if you remember to remove the ice cream to the fridge just before dinner.

Iced Orange Cream

This is a smooth, rich very orangey iced cream – the lemon rind and juice isn't detectable as lemon, it accentuates the orange. We serve it with warm chocolate sauce. It benefits from being made in the ice cream machine, or by a couple of good beatings as it freezes.

Serves 6–8

8 egg yolks	*juice of 1 lemon*
8 oz (225 g) caster sugar	*juice of 2 oranges*
grated rind of 1 lemon	*½ pint (300 ml) double*
grated rind of 3 oranges	*cream*

22

Whisk the egg yolks, gradually adding the caster sugar, until they are very pale and thick. Whisk in the rinds of the lemon and oranges and the juice of the lemon.

Whip the cream, gradually whipping into it the juice of 2 oranges. Fold together the two mixtures, pour into a polythene container and freeze. Take it out of the deep freeze after 1½–2 hours, and beat it thoroughly; put it back into the deep freeze and beat again after a further couple of hours. Alternatively, if you have an ice cream machine, pour it into the machine and churn-freeze for 25 minutes, then scrape it into a polythene container and put in the deep freeze. Remove from the deep freeze and leave at room temperature for 30 minutes before serving.

Nesselrode Ice Cream

This is a sort of Christmas pudding ice, quite delicious and extremely popular around Christmas and New Year.

Serves 8

---

2 oz (50 g) glacé cherries
4 oz (125 g) raisins
4 tablespoons brandy or rum
½ pint (300 ml) single
    cream
4 oz (125 g) plain chocolate
4 egg yolks
2 oz (50 g) caster sugar
7-oz (200-g) tin
    unsweetened chestnut
purée (if you can only get
    sweetened, leave out the
    sugar)
2 oz (50 g) flaked almonds,
    toasted
½ pint (300 ml) double
    cream, whipped but not
    too stiffly

Chop the cherries roughly and put them and the raisins to soak in the brandy or rum while you make the rest of the mixture. Put the single cream into a heavy saucepan over a gentle heat, and break the chocolate into it. Heat until the chocolate has melted in the cream. Meanwhile, beat together the egg yolks and caster sugar. Pour a little of the hot chocolate cream on to the yolks mixture and mix well. Pour on the rest of the cream, then return it all to the heavy saucepan and cook, stirring continuously, over a gentle heat until the custard coats the back of your wooden spoon. Remove from the heat and beat in the chestnut purée. Then stir in the cherries, raisins and brandy, and the toasted flaked almonds. Leave to get completely cold, then fold this mixture into the whipped cream. Pour it into a polythene container and freeze. Remove from the freezer and leave at room temperature for 30 minutes before serving.

Baked Alaska

This is a real celebration pud. It is also most convenient because it is made entirely several days ahead and frozen. To serve, it needs only to be popped into a hot oven for 15 minutes and set alight, which adds a touch of drama to the proceedings. At the same time it deliciously toasts the almonds dotting the meringue surface and caramelises the sugar sprinkled over it. For the ice cream, use either of the recipes given on pages 14 and 15. I tend to make the first one for this, because I can then use the egg whites for the meringue.

Serves 8–10

Vanilla Ice Cream 1 or 2 (page 14 or 15)
Sponge cake base:
3 eggs
3 oz (75 g) caster sugar
3 oz (75 g) self-raising flour, sieved twice

Meringue:
6 egg whites
10 oz (275 g) caster sugar
For finishing:
2 oz (50 g) flaked almonds
1 rounded tablespoon granulated sugar
3 tablespoons brandy

Make the ice cream first. Then line an oblong baking tin, about 8 by 12 in (20.5 by 30 cm) with siliconised paper. Break the eggs into a bowl and whisk (I use a hand-held electric whisk) gradually adding the caster sugar. Whisk until the mixture is really thick and almost white – this takes 7–10 minutes. The mixture should hold its shape when you trail a squiggle on its surface. Then, quickly and thoroughly, fold in the twice-sieved flour. Pour it into the prepared tin and bake for 15–20 minutes in a moderate oven, 350°F (180°C) Gas mark 4 (bottom right-hand oven in a 4-door Aga). Remove from the oven and cool on a wire rack.

At this point I must warn you of a pitfall (into which I once fell, needless to say!). Whatever you put the Baked Alaska on has to be suitable for freezing and then for putting straight from the freezer into a very hot oven; I use a large baking tray.

Put the cold sponge on the baking tray or a large flat dish and spoon the frozen ice cream over the sponge, leaving about 1 in (2.5 cm) around the sides. Put this into the freezer.

Whisk the egg whites until very stiff, then gradually whisk in all the sugar. Take the baking tray with the sponge and ice cream out of the freezer and quickly cover the entire surface with the meringue. Make the meringue cover everything – right over the sides of the sponge. Strew the flaked almonds over the surface and put the whole thing, uncovered, back into the freezer. When it has had 2 or 3 hours in the freezer, carefully cover it with a piece of foil – I say carefully, because the frozen meringue never goes completely hard. Try not to squash it with anything else in the freezer.

Thirty minutes or so before you are ready to serve it, take the Baked Alaska out of the freezer. Fifteen minutes later sprinkle the granulated sugar over the surface and put it in a hot oven, 400°F (200°C) Gas mark 6 (top right-hand oven in a 4-door Aga) for 15 minutes. Meanwhile, gently warm the brandy. I do this in a large soup ladle, but a small saucepan does just as well, as long as the brandy doesn't boil. Just before you take the Baked Alaska to the table, set the brandy alight and pour it flaming over the surface of the Alaska. Blow the flames out before things get too charred, and serve immediately.

Raspberry Ice Cream

Serves 8

---

3 eggs, separated	½ pint (300 ml) double
3 oz (75 g) icing sugar,	cream
sieved	1 pint (600 ml) raspberry
	purée, approximately

Make the raspberry purée by cooking the raspberries just until their juices run, then liquidising and sieving them.

Whisk the egg whites, gradually adding nearly all the sieved icing sugar and whisking until the meringue is stiff and peaky. Whisk the yolks with the remaining sugar, until quite pale. Whip the cream, but not too stiffly. Fold the yolks, meringue and raspberry purée together, and taste. If you think this isn't sweet enough, sieve a little more icing sugar into the whipped cream before folding this into the raspberry mixture. Pour it into a polythene container and freeze.

Take it out of the freezer after a couple of hours, and beat the mixture well. Return it to the freezer then beat again after another 1½–2 hours. If you have an ice cream machine, put the prepared raspberry cream into it, and churn-freeze for 25 minutes, then put the resulting ice cream into a polythene container and freeze. Remove from the freezer and leave at room temperature for about 30 minutes before serving.

Iced Plum, Cinnamon & Port Parfait

This is more of a frozen mousse than an ice cream. The cinnamon and port, whilst scarcely detectable in themselves, combine with the plums to make a really exquisite flavour. Don't make it with Victoria plums, which are so good to eat; they are a dessert fruit, but cooked seem to lose their attraction. Any of the other yellow or dark red, rather sharp-tasting plums are ideal.

Serves 8

---

1 lb (450 g) plums
2 wine glasses port
1 rounded tablespoon
  granulated sugar

1 rounded dessertspoon
  ground cinnamon
3 eggs, separated
3 oz (75 g) caster sugar
½ pint (300 ml) double
  cream

Put the plums into a heavy saucepan, pour on half the port, add the granulated sugar, and cover the pan with a lid. Put the pan on a moderate heat, and cook until the plums are soft. Remove from the heat and remove the stones. Then, using a slotted spoon, put the plums together with the cinnamon in a liquidiser and blend to a purée. If the plums have made a lot of juice, don't add it all, because the purée will be too runny. Leave to get cold.

Whisk the egg yolks and gradually add the caster sugar, whisking until they are very pale and thick. Fold the cooled purée into them. Whip the cream and remaining port together, not too stiffly, and fold the cream into the plum

27

mixture. Lastly, whisk the egg whites stiffly, and fold them in, using a metal spoon. Pour into a polythene container and freeze. Remove from the freezer and leave at room temperature for 30 minutes before serving.

Vanilla & Chocolate Mint Crisp Ice Cream

Children go wild in anticipation of this particular ice cream, and with the prospect of it for pudding can be bribed to do anything. I find that so-called grown-ups love it equally, especially if the lily is well and truly gilded by serving it with chocolate sauce. The better the mint crisps the better the ice cream; my favourite are Elizabeth Shaw's, but you can use half and half plain and milk chocolate with something like Mint Matchsticks.

Serves 8

---

8 oz (225 g) chocolate mint crisps
4 eggs, separated
3 oz (75 g) icing sugar, sieved

½ pint (300 ml) double cream, whipped, but not too stiffly

If you have a food processor, pulverise the chocolate crisps in it. If you don't, bash them in a bowl with the end of a rolling pin into bits as small as possible. Whisk the egg whites until just beginning to be peaky, then whisk in the sieved icing sugar. Whisk until stiff.

Whisk the egg yolks, and whisk them into the whipped cream. Fold together the meringue, the cream and yolks mixture and the pulverised mint crisps, pour into a polythene container and freeze.

Remove from the freezer and leave at room temperature

for 30 minutes before serving.

If you have an ice cream maker, churn-freeze the mixture for 25 minutes then scrape this into a container and freeze.

Clementine Water Ice

The flavour of clementines is delicate and exquisite, making a lovely, refreshing finale to a rich winter's dinner. The more this or any water ice is beaten as it freezes, the better will be the end result. Water ices can be like ice lollies – just one giant rock-hard crystal. If they are beaten as they freeze, the texture becomes soft and the volume increases, the colour becomes more opaque, and they are easier to both serve and eat.

Serves 4–6

---

*4 oz (125 g) granulated
   sugar
pared rind of 1 lemon and 3
   clementines*

*juice of 1 lemon and 5
   clementines*

Put ½ pint (300 ml) water, the sugar and pared rinds together in a saucepan over a moderate heat. Heat until the sugar has dissolved completely, then boil fast for 4–5 minutes. Remove from the heat, add the squeezed juices, and leave to get completely cold. Then fish out the rinds. Pour the liquid into a container and freeze.

After about 1–1½ hours, remove from the freezer and either tip into a food processor and whizz, then return to the freezer, or whisk hard and return to the freezer. Repeat this at least 3 times.

Alternatively, if you have an ice cream maker, churn-freeze for 20 minutes, which gives a perfect result, then keep the water ice in the deep freeze.

Transfer the ice to the fridge 30 minutes before serving.

Geranium Leaf Water Ice

This is another refreshing fragrant water ice, flavoured with geranium leaves. You can substitute elderflowers for the geranium leaves.

Serves 4

---

6 oz (175 g) granulated sugar
pared rind of 1 lemon

a good handful of geranium leaves
juice of 1 lemon

Put 1 pint (600 ml) water, the sugar and pared lemon rind into a saucepan over a moderate heat until the sugar has dissolved completely, then boil rapidly for 5 minutes. Draw the saucepan off the heat and put the geranium leaves into the hot syrup. Leave to cool completely, then fish out the leaves and add the lemon juice. Pour into a container and freeze.

After $1-1\frac{1}{2}$ hours remove from the freezer and beat well, either by tipping it into a food processor and whizzing, or by hand beating. Replace in the container, and return to the freezer. Repeat this beating twice more, at intervals of about $1\frac{1}{2}$ hours. If you have an ice cream maker put the mixture in to churn-freeze for 20 minutes, then put it in the freezer. Transfer to the fridge for 30 minutes before serving.

Lemon & Raspberry Water Ice

My favourite water ice of all, I think, or perhaps it ties for first place with elderflower water ice.

Serves 6

---

pared rind of 2 lemons
5 oz (150 g) granulated sugar
juice of 2 lemons
about 1 pint (600 ml) raspberry purée, made from raspberries which

have been cooked just until their juices run, then liquidised, and sieved to remove the little woody pips

---

Put ½ pint (300 ml) water, the pared lemon rinds and granulated sugar into a saucepan over a moderate heat, until the sugar has completely dissolved. Then boil rapidly for 5 minutes. Draw off the heat, and cool.

When the syrup is quite cold, fish out the bits of rind, stir in the lemon juice and raspberry purée, and pour into a polythene container to freeze. After about 1–1½ hours, remove the container from the freezer and beat the contents well. Put the container back into the freezer, and repeat the beating process twice more, at intervals of about 1½ hours. If you have a food processor, whizz the mixture in it, instead of beating. If you have an ice cream maker, put the mixture in to churn-freeze for 20 minutes, then freeze it. Transfer to the fridge for 30 minutes before serving.

Fresh Lime Water Ice

This makes a lovely change from the more usual lemon water ice. Our adventurous fruit and vegetable wholesaler, Norman Macleod in Portree, is always receptive to requests and limes have become a weekly order during the summer.

Serves 6

---

pared rind of 4 limes　　　　*juice of 4 limes*
5 oz (150 g) granulated
*　sugar*

Put 1 pint (600 ml) water, the pared lime rinds and sugar together in a saucepan over a moderate heat, until the sugar has dissolved completely. Then boil rapidly for 5 minutes. Remove from the heat, and cool. Fish out the bits of rind and pour in the lime juice. Pour into a polythene container and freeze for 1–1½ hours, then take it out of the freezer and beat well. Return it to the freezer and repeat this beating process twice. If you have a food processor you can whizz the semi-frozen ice in that, instead of beating. If you have an ice cream maker, pour in the mixture and churn-freeze for 20 minutes, then scoop into a container and freeze. Transfer to the fridge for 30 minutes before serving.

Crêpes

S weet pancakes – *crêpes* (such panache to that word) –
make a lovely pudding. They can be very convenient
too, as in some recipes you can freeze the entire dish,
just thawing and reheating it when you want it. Pancakes
are a bit of a fiddle to make, but they are so appreciated
that I don't begrudge a moment spent on them.

Sweet pancakes can be either hot, as in the recipes for
Cinnamon Crêpes with Apricot and Chestnut Filling, and
Crêpes Suzette, or cold. For serving cold, I think they are
best not frozen, but they are fine made a day ahead.

Basic Pancakes, Served with Lemon Wedges & Caster Sugar

Makes 16, Serves 8

4 oz (125 g) plain flour	*a little more butter for frying*
1 oz (25 g) caster sugar	*the pancakes*
¼ pint (150 ml) milk	For serving :
¼ pint (150 ml) water	*lemon juice*
2 large eggs	*lemon wedges*
2 tablespoons melted butter	*caster sugar*

Put all the ingredients except the butter for frying into a liquidiser or food processor and whizz until smooth. Leave for an hour or two before you make up the pancakes.

The ideal-sized pan for pancakes is about 7 in (18 cm) in diameter. I have a super pan which I keep for pancakes and omelettes only, and which I just wipe out with kitchen paper after using.

When you are ready to cook, heat the pancake pan over a moderate heat, with about ½ oz (15 g) butter in it. When the butter is foaming, pour in a little pancake batter, swirling it around the pan so that a thin layer covers the base. Cook for 1–2 minutes, then turn it over and cook the other side – I find the easiest way to turn a pancake over is with my fingers, taking care not to burn them in the process! Sprinkle each cooked pancake with lemon juice and caster sugar, and roll them up like cigars. Keep them warm on a plate until you are ready to serve them. Serve them with lemon wedges around the edge of the serving plate.

Crêpes with Praline Whipped Cream

These really are delectable, extremely fattening, and worth every calorie.

Serves 8

---

16 pancakes (page 36)
3 oz (75 g) granulated
    sugar
2 oz (50 g) almonds, whole
    or flaked

¾ pint (425 ml) double
    cream, whipped fairly
    stiffly
icing sugar
Fudge Sauce (page 157)

Make up the pancakes and leave to cool. Put the sugar and almonds together in a saucepan over a moderate heat and melt the sugar, shaking the pan as the sugar begins to dissolve. When the sugar has all dissolved, and is a rich golden brown (but not black brown – burnt caramel has such a bitter taste) pour it on to a well greased tin to cool and harden. When it is quite cold, cover it with a piece of greaseproof paper and bash it with a rolling pin into fairly fine crumbs. Stir this into the whipped cream.

Lay each cooked and cooled pancake out. Divide the praline cream between the pancakes, roll up, and arrange on a serving dish. Dust with sieved icing sugar before serving with warm fudge sauce.

Lemon Crêpes with Raspberry & Lemon Cream Filling

I love the flavour of lemon and raspberries – one enhances the other. This pudding can be made using well drained frozen raspberries.

Serves 8

---

4 oz (125 g) plain flour
1 oz (25 g) caster sugar
¼ pint (150 ml) milk
¼ pint (150 ml) water
2 large eggs
2 tablespoons melted butter
grated rind of 1 lemon
icing sugar for dusting

Filling:
½ pint (300 ml) double
    cream, whipped fairly
    stiffly
2 oz (50 g) caster sugar
finely grated rind of 1 lemon
1 lb (450 g) raspberries

Make up the batter as for Basic Pancakes (page 36), adding the lemon rind. Make 16 pancakes and leave to cool.

Stir the sugar and lemon rind into the whipped cream, and then stir in the raspberries. Lay each cooked and cooled crêpe out and divide the raspberry cream filling between them. Roll them up and arrange on a serving dish. Dust with icing sugar before serving.

Cinnamon Crêpes with Apricot & Chestnut Filling

Serves 8

4 oz (125 g) plain flour
1 oz (25 g) caster sugar
¼ pint (150 ml) milk
¼ pint (150 ml) water
2 large eggs
2 tablespoons melted butter
1 rounded dessertspoon
   cinnamon
icing sugar for dusting

½ pint (300 ml) double
   cream, whipped
Filling:
1 lb (450 g) good apricot
   jam
1-lb (450-g) tin
   unsweetened chestnut
   purée

Make up the batter as for Basic Pancakes (page 36), adding the cinnamon. Make 16 pancakes.

Tip the jam and the unsweetened chestnut purée into a bowl and, using a wooden spoon, break them down and work them together until they are smooth. The drawback to doing this in a food processor is that you get a perfectly smooth purée, whereas I like small chunks of apricot in the filling. Divide the mixture between the cooked crêpes, roll them up and arrange them on an ovenproof serving dish. Dust with sieved icing sugar, and pop them into a moderate oven, 350°F (180°C) Gas mark 4 (bottom right-hand oven of a 4-door Aga) for 20 minutes. Serve with whipped cream.

My Version of Crêpes Suzette

This is a lovely, warming dish, a perfect finale to a winter dinner party.

Serves 8

---

4 oz (125 g) plain flour
1 oz (25 g) caster sugar
¼ pint (150 ml) water
¼ pint (150 ml) milk
2 large eggs
2 tablespoons melted butter
grated rind of 1 orange
Filling:
4 oz (125 g) butter

4 oz (125 g) icing sugar,
  sieved
grated rind of 1 orange
4 tablespoons brandy, or
  orange liqueur
For finishing:
1–2 tablespoons icing sugar
3 tablespoons brandy

Make up the batter as for Basic Pancakes (page 36), adding the orange rind. Make 16 pancakes and leave them to cool. Put the butter for the filling into a bowl and cream it together with the sieved icing sugar and orange rind. If you have a food processor you can do all this in it and the icing sugar need not be sieved. Very gradually, almost teaspoon by teaspoon, beat in the brandy or orange liqueur.

Spread out the cooked pancakes, and divide the butter-cream evenly between them. Spread it out to make a thin covering over each pancake, and fold each in half, then in half again, to form a triangle. Butter a large ovenproof dish, and arrange the triangles overlapping in it. If you are going to freeze the dish, do so now, covering it with foil or cling film.

When you remove the dish from the deep freeze, leave it at room temperature for 2–3 hours, then carry on, as if you hadn't frozen it.

Dust all over with sieved icing sugar, and put the dish in a low oven, 250°F (130°C) Gas mark 1 (top left-hand oven in a 4-door Aga) for 20 minutes, or until the buttery filling has melted. Warm the extra brandy in a small saucepan (don't let it boil!) and just before you are ready to serve, ignite the brandy in the pan, and pour the flaming brandy over the crêpes. Blow out the flames before the crêpes scorch, and serve with whipped cream for those who like it.

Pastry Puddings

I must admit that until I bought my first food processor, many years ago, I was the frozen pastry manufacturer's best customer. Then Peter and I devised a very rich, short pastry which has no liquid or egg added, and which is patted round the sides of the tin or flan dish in its crumb-like state. It sounds odd, but it is delicious. It is also versatile, as the pastry can include nuts, as in the recipe for Blackcurrant and Hazelnut Tart, or it can be a fudgey digestive biscuit base, as in the Bavarian Cheesecake.

The choice of the best pie depends on what precedes it in the menu – the fruity pies are refreshing, whereas Butter-scotch Tart and Chocolate and Rum Pie nicely round off a menu which has contained light preceding courses.

Butterscotch Tart

Serves 6–8

Pastry:
4 oz (125 g) butter hard
 from the fridge
5 oz (150 g) plain flour
1 oz (25 g) icing sugar
Butterscotch filling:
8 oz (225 g) soft brown
 sugar

4 oz (125 g) butter
2 eggs
4 egg yolks
1 level tablespoon cornflour
2 14.5-fl oz (412-ml) tins
 evaporated milk
1½ teaspoons vanilla essence

Cut the butter in bits into the bowl of a food processor. Put the flour and icing sugar in with the butter, and whizz until the mixture resembles breadcrumbs. If you do not have a food processor, cut the butter into the flour and icing sugar with a knife, then use your fingers to rub the mixture to a breadcrumb-like texture. Pat this mixture around the inside of a flan dish about 8 in (20 cm) in diameter, and put the dish in the fridge for at least 30 minutes, the longer the better. Then bake in a moderate oven, 350°F (180°C) Gas mark 4 (bottom right-hand oven in a 4-door Aga) for about 30 minutes, until the pastry is evenly cooked and a pale biscuit colour.

Put the butter and brown sugar together in a saucepan, and heat them gently together until the sugar is dissolved, then boil for 5 minutes. In a bowl, mix well together the eggs, yolks and cornflour, gradually adding one tin of evaporated milk. Pour the contents of the other tin of milk into the saucepan with the butterscotch, but be careful doing this, as the steam whooshes up from the bubbling butterscotch. The butterscotch in the saucepan will dissolve into the evaporated milk.

Then pour a little of the hot liquid from the pan on to the contents of the bowl, mix well and pour it back into the saucepan. Over a moderate heat, stir continuously until the mixture boils. If it seems a bit thick for your liking, add a little fresh milk. When it has boiled, remove the saucepan from the heat and stir in the vanilla essence. Leave until quite cold, and then sieve the filling on to the cooled rich pastry case. Smooth the surface all over and decorate, if you like, with a sprinkling of grated dark chocolate.

Chocolate & Rum Pie

This is a creamy, chocolatey pie which freezes satisfactorily, but not for too long, not much more than 3 weeks.

Serves 6–8

pastry (page 44)	1 rounded teaspoon cornflour
½ pint (300 ml) milk	1 level dessertspoon gelatine
½ teaspoon nutmeg, freshly grated if possible	sprinkled over 3 tablespoons cold water
4 oz (125 g) dark chocolate	4 fl oz (125 ml) rum
3 eggs, separated	½ pint (300 ml) double cream
4 oz (125 g) caster sugar	

Prepare an 8 in (20 cm) pastry case, as for Butterscotch Tart (page 44). Put the milk and nutmeg into a saucepan and break the chocolate into it. Put the pan over a gentle heat and stir occasionally until the chocolate has melted. Beat the egg yolks, sugar and cornflour together until creamy, pour on to them a little of the hot chocolatey milk, mix well, and pour the lot back into the pan. Put the saucepan back on a gentle heat and stir continuously until the custard has thickened enough to coat the back of the wooden spoon, to the extent that when you draw your

45

finger down the back of the spoon a clear path is left through the coating of custard. This will take about 10 minutes, but I try not to rush and turn up the heat, which would result in a curdled mess, nor to persuade myself that the custard has thickened enough when it is still too runny; it just needs patience, and it is worth it.

When you take the pan of thickened chocolatey custard off the heat, stir in the soaked gelatine. Stir until it dissolves and then stir in the rum. Leave to cool completely.

Whip the cream until thick and just beginning to stand in soft peaks when you lift the whisk out. Fold this into the cold chocolate custard. Whisk 2 egg whites until very stiff and, using a metal spoon, fold them into the creamy custard. Pour this into the baked pastry shell, and leave in a cool place to set.

Spiced Raisin Cream Pie

This spicy, creamy pie, full of raisins, is enjoyed by all who eat it, but by no one more than Hugo, our youngest.

Serves 6–8

---

pastry (page 44)	*8 oz (225 g) raisins*
3 eggs, separated	*¼ pint (150 ml) double*
4 oz (125 g) caster sugar	*cream*
1 rounded teaspoon cornflour	*grated rind of 1 lemon and 1*
1 level teaspoon ground	*orange*
cinnamon	*juice of ½ a lemon*
½ teaspoon grated nutmeg	
(freshly grated if	
possible)	

Prepare an 8 in (20 cm) pastry case, as for Butterscotch Tart (page 44). Beat together the egg yolks, caster sugar, cornflour and the spices. Beat until creamy. Stir in the raisins, cream, lemon and orange rinds, and the lemon juice. Whisk the egg whites until stiff and, using a metal spoon, fold them into the yolk mixture. Pour into the baked pastry case and bake in a moderate oven, 350°F (180°C) Gas mark 4 (bottom right-hand oven of a 4-door Aga) for 30–35 minutes. Remove from the oven and eat while still warm.

Bavarian Cheesecake

This cheesecake recipe is the best and quickest that I've come across. It was given to me years ago by Caroline Fox. It is delicious just as it is, but you can also adapt it to become a fruity cheesecake, by arranging halved strawberries, blackcurrants or blackberries on top.

Serves 6–8

Cheesecake base:
10 digestive biscuits crushed into crumbs
3 oz (75 g) melted butter
Cheesecake filling:
12 oz (350 g) cottage or cream cheese
4 oz (125 g) icing sugar, sieved

1 rounded dessertspoon gelatine, dissolved in 4 tablespoons water over a gentle heat
½ pint (300 ml) double cream
grated rind of either 2 lemons or 2 oranges
3 egg whites

To make the biscuits into crumbs, put them in a polythene bag and bash and roll with a rolling pin, it saves mess. Mix the biscuit crumbs and melted butter together and pat round the sides and bottom of an 8 in (20 cm) flan dish. Put the flan dish into a moderate oven, 350°F (180°C) Gas mark 4 (bottom right-hand oven in a 4-door Aga) for 15 minutes. Remove from the oven, and cool. If you have a food processor, put in the cream cheese, 1 oz (25 g) icing sugar and the gelatine dissolved in water and whizz. If you don't have a food processor, mix these ingredients together in a bowl, using a wooden spoon to get the mixture as smooth as possible. Whip the cream till thick and stir into it the lemon or orange rinds. Whisk the egg whites until stiff then, spoonful by spoonful, whisk in the remaining 3 oz (75 g) icing sugar, whisking until stiff.

Using a spatula, scrape the cheese and gelatine mixture from the food processor or bowl into the whipped cream, and fold the mixtures together. Using a metal spoon, fold the meringue into the creamy mixture. Pour this into the flan dish, on top of the baked digestive biscuit base. Leave in a cool place to set.

Fresh Lime Pie

This rich pie, with its sharp filling of limes and its buttery texture, makes a stunning finale to a dinner.

Serves 6–8

---

pastry (page 44)	*4 oz (125 g) butter*
6 limes	To decorate:
4 eggs	*2 limes, cut into thin slices*
8 oz (125 g) caster sugar	

Prepare an 8 in (20 cm) flan case, as for Butterscotch Tart (page 44). Grate the lime rind into a bowl and add the eggs, sugar and butter. Put the bowl over a saucepan of gently simmering water and stir with a spoon or a whisk until the butter has melted and the sugar dissolved.

Remove the bowl from the pan. Squeeze the juice from the limes and stir the juice into the contents of the bowl.

Pour this mixture into the baked pastry case, and carefully put it into a low oven, 300°F (150°C) Gas mark 2 (bottom of the bottom right-hand oven in a 4-door Aga). Cook for about 15 minutes, until the filling is just set to the touch – it shouldn't change colour at all. Remove from the oven. Decorate with thin slices of lime, cut in half and placed side by side around the edge of the pie, the straight side of each half facing the edge of the dish.

Plum & Almond Tart

The crunch of the flaked or nibbed almonds in this pastry makes a good contrast in texture through the soft plums.

Serves 6–8

Pastry:	Plum filling:
4 oz (125 g) butter straight from the fridge	*2 lb (1 kg) plums*
	sugar to taste
4 oz (125 g) plain flour	*1 rounded tablespoon*
1 oz (25 g) icing sugar	*arrowroot, or cornflour*
2 oz (50 g) flaked or nibbed almonds	

If you have a food processor, put the butter, cut up in bits, into the processor, then add the flour and icing sugar. Whizz until the mixture resembles breadcrumbs. Stir the flaked or nibbed almonds through the mixture – remember not to put them in the food processor, as they pulverise down and you lose the crunch.

If you are making the pastry by hand, put the butter, flour and icing sugar into a bowl, and cut the butter into the flour and sugar, until the butter is in small bits. Use your finger tips to rub the mixture into a breadcrumb-like consistency and stir in the almonds.

Make a case in an 8 in (20 cm) flan dish, as on page 44.

Cut the plums in half and put them into a saucepan with 1 tablespoon water and about 2 oz (50 g) sugar. Put the pan on a gentle to moderate heat, with a lid on. Cook gently until the plums are soft, they will make a lot of juice. Remove the pan from the heat and, using a slotted spoon and a fork, remove the stones, which will mostly have obligingly come to the surface. Add more sugar if necessary and stir to dissolve it.

Put the arrowroot in a cup or a small bowl. (Arrowroot really is better to use for thickening fruit syrups such as this, because as it boils it becomes clear, leaving the fruit sauce jewel-like. Cornflour will do, but the sauce will be slightly cloudy.) Slake it with a little cold water, mix it till smooth, then add a little of the juice from the saucepan. Pour the arrowroot mixture into the saucepan, replace the pan on the heat and stir until it boils and thickens. Remove the pan from the heat and leave to cool completely before pouring into the cold almond pastry case. Serve with whipped cream.

Strawberry Crème Pâtissière Pie

This spectacular pie tastes just as good as it looks. It is a pie for an occasion: a birthday, an anniversary, or some such celebration.

Serves 6–8

---

pastry (page 44)
½ pint (300 ml) milk
3 egg yolks
2 oz (50 g) caster sugar
1 rounded teaspoon cornflour
few drops of vanilla essence
½ pint (300 ml) double
* cream*

1 lb (450 g) strawberries
4 tablespoons redcurrant
* jelly, warmed in a small*
* saucepan and beaten with*
* a wooden spoon until quite*
* smooth*

Prepare an 8 in (20 cm) flan case, as for Butterscotch Tart (page 44). Put the milk into a saucepan over a gentle heat and warm. Put the egg yolks, caster sugar and cornflour into a bowl and beat well. Pour a little of the hot milk on to the egg yolk mixture and mix well, then pour this all back into the saucepan with the rest of the milk. Over a gentle heat, stir continuously until the mixture is just about to boil – when it first starts to heave gently. Remove from the heat and stir in the vanilla essence. Cool and sieve. Whip the cream and fold it and the cold, sieved custard together. Pour this crème pâtissière into the cold cooked pastry case.

Hull the strawberries and cut in half. Arrange the halved strawberries in ever-decreasing circles, starting at the outside edge of the flan and working towards the centre; or alternatively you can arrange them in lines across. When the whole pie surface is covered with strawberries, using a pastry brush, gently brush the entire surface of each strawberry, the edge of the pastry – the lot – with the smooth redcurrant jelly. This sounds a fiddle, but it is worth doing, because suddenly the pie becomes extremely professional in appearance. The cries of appreciation that greet it are out of all proportion to the time involved in doing it!

Apple & Mincemeat Meringue Pie

Now this is one of my favourite of all pies. With our own version of rich pastry, the orange, brandy, mincemeat and apple centre, and the soft meringue top, there is really everything in it to satisfy my sweet tooth!

Serves 6–8

---

pastry (page 44)
4 large cooking apples, about
    1½–2 lb (700–900 g),
    when peeled and cored
1 oz (25 g) butter
grated rind of 2 oranges and
    1 lemon
2 rounded tablespoons soft
    brown sugar
1 lb (450 g) mincemeat,
    home-made if possible

4 tablespoons brandy – this
    is purely optional, fresh
    orange juice can be
    substituted, but the
    brandy does give rather a
    nice kick
Meringue:
3 egg whites
6 oz (175 g) caster sugar

Prepare an 8 in (20 cm) flan case, as for Butterscotch Tart (page 44). Peel, core and chop the cooking apples. Melt the butter in a saucepan, and add the chopped apples. Add 4 tablespoons water, the grated orange and lemon rinds and the soft brown sugar, and stir all together. Cover the saucepan with a lid and put the pan over a gentle to moderate heat. Cook gently until the apples are soft and broken down – about 30 minutes. Remove from the heat and cool. Stir the mincemeat and brandy into the apple mixture, and spoon evenly into the flan case. In a bowl, whisk the egg whites until fairly stiff then, whisking all the time, add the caster sugar spoonful by spoonful. Whisk until it is all incorporated and the meringue is nice and stiff. Spoon this over the apple and mincemeat filling, taking the meringue right over the edges of the pastry all around the pie. Bake in a low to moderate oven, 325°F (170°C) Gas mark 3 (bottom of the bottom right-hand oven of a 4-door Aga) for 30 minutes. Remove from the oven and eat warm, with whipped cream.

On a chilly winter's evening, this pie has brought cries of admiration from even the most convinced non-pudding eaters!

Blackcurrant & Hazelnut Tart

This tart combines the lovely flavour and slightly crunchy texture of hazelnuts in the pastry, with the, to me, heavenly flavour of blackcurrants. The juice is thickened very slightly, to avoid making the pastry soggy and to make serving a decent slice of pie possible. Choose a brand of blackcurrant brandy that is not too sweet, or plain brandy will do. Or you can leave the alcohol out altogether.

Serves 6–8

Pastry:	Filling:
4 oz (125 g) butter, hard from the fridge	*2 lb (1 kg) blackcurrants*
3 oz (75 g) plain flour	*3–4 oz (75–125 g) caster sugar*
3 oz (75 g) ground hazelnuts	*1 rounded tablespoon arrowroot, or cornflour*
1 oz (25 g) icing sugar	*4 fl oz (125 ml) blackcurrant brandy, or brandy, optional*

53

If you have a food processor, cut the butter into it, add the flour, ground hazelnuts and icing sugar, and whizz until the mixture is like breadcrumbs. If you don't have a processor, cut the butter into a bowl, add the flour, hazelnuts and icing sugar, and continue cutting until the butter is in quite tiny bits. Use your finger tips to rub the mixture to a breadcrumb-like consistency. Pat this mixture round the sides and bottom of an 8 in (20 cm) flan dish, and put in the fridge for at least 30 minutes, or as long as possible. Then bake in a moderate oven, 350°F (180°C) Gas mark 4 (middle shelf of the bottom right-hand oven of a 4-door Aga) for about 30 minutes, until the pastry is evenly cooked and a golden biscuity colour. Remove from the oven, and cool.

Put the blackcurrants (topped and tailed) into a saucepan together with $\frac{1}{4}$ pint (150 ml) water and the sugar, and cover the pan with a lid. Simmer very gently for 20 minutes, stirring occasionally until the sugar has dissolved.

Put the arrowroot or cornflour into a small bowl, and slake with a couple of tablespoons of water; pour a little of the juice from the saucepan into the bowl and mix well, then pour this back into the pan with the blackcurrants and the rest of the juice. Over a moderate heat, stir the contents until the sauce thickens and boils. Remove from the heat, cool a little, then stir in the blackcurrant brandy, or plain brandy. When the blackcurrant mixture is quite cold, pour it into the baked hazelnut pastry case, smoothing the surface. Serve with slightly sweetened whipped cream.

Pecan (or Walnut) Pie

This is a very rich pie, absolutely delicious. It is best of all made with pecan nuts, which are becoming easier and easier to get in Britain – I can even buy them in Inverness. But if you can't find any, substitute walnuts instead.

Serves 6–8

---

pastry (page 44)
4 oz (125 g) butter
4 oz (125 g) soft brown
sugar
2 tablespoons golden syrup –
measure this by dipping
the tablespoon in a jug of

very hot water before
spooning the syrup, the
syrup will then slip easily
off the spoon
4 eggs, well beaten
6 oz (175 g) shelled pecans,
or walnuts

Prepare an 8 in (20 cm) flan case, as for Butterscotch Tart (page 44). Just put the rest of the ingredients except the nuts into a bowl over a pan of simmering water, and stir until the butter is melted and the sugar dissolved. Carefully pour this into the baked pastry case, and put the nuts evenly over the top – they will sink into the liquid. Bake the pie in a low to moderate oven, 325°F (170°C) Gas mark 3 (bottom of the bottom right-hand oven of a 4-door Aga) for about 20 minutes, or until the filling is just firm to the touch. Remove from the oven. I like to serve this pie warm, with whipped cream.

Chocolate Cream Cheese Pie

This pie manages to be light as well as creamy and rich, and it freezes very successfully. Being chocolate, it is, of course, right up my street!

Serves 6–8

Biscuit base:	*8 oz (225 g) cream cheese*
10 dark chocolate wholemeal	*4 oz (125 g) caster sugar*
biscuits, crushed finely	*1 teaspoon vanilla essence*
3 oz (75 g) butter, melted	*2 eggs, separated*
Filling:	*¼ pint (150 ml) double*
6 oz (175 g) dark chocolate	*cream*

Mix the chocolate biscuit crumbs and the melted butter together, and press round the sides and bottom of a flan dish about 8 in (20 cm) in diameter. Bake in a moderate oven, 350°F (180°C) Gas mark 4 (bottom right-hand oven of a 4-door Aga) for about 15 minutes. Remove from the oven, and cool.

Break the chocolate into a bowl and place over a pan of simmering water until melted. If you have a food processor, put the cream cheese, caster sugar and vanilla essence into it and whizz until smooth. If you don't have a processor, do this in a mixing bowl using a wooden spoon to break the cheese down and mix it into the sugar, getting it as smooth as possible. Beat in the egg yolks, one by one, beating really well. Next beat in the cooled melted chocolate. Whip the cream and fold it into the chocolate mixture. Lastly, whisk the egg whites until stiff and fold them in using a metal spoon. Pour and spoon this mixture into the cold chocolate pie base, and leave in a cool place until you are ready to serve it.

Steamed Bramble &
Lemon Suet Pudding

To many people, suet puddings are still redolent of institutions. This is really sad, because a good steamed pud, as long as it has a generous and flavour-packed filling, really beats a fruit pie. It is easy to make, too. This is real Sunday lunch stuff, and is always greatly appreciated. Lemon and blackberries go together extremely well, and in this pudding there is also butter and brown sugar – the combined flavours are heavenly.

I use this quantity of suet pastry to line a pudding bowl about 3 pints (1.7 l) in size.

Serves 6–8

Pastry:	*6 oz (175 g) soft brown*
8 oz (225 g) plain flour	*sugar*
½ teaspoon baking powder	*grated rind of 3 lemons*
4 oz (125 g) shredded suet	*3 oz (75 g) butter, cut in*
Filling:	*bits*
1½ lb (800 g) blackberries	

Mix all the pastry ingredients together with enough cold water to make a dough and knead a bit. Cut about one quarter of the pastry off and set aside (this is for the lid). Roll the remaining pastry out. Lightly butter the inside of a 3 pint (1.7 litre) pudding basin – you can now get plastic bowls with snap-on lids and handles on top of the lids which take all the hard work out of preparing a bowl for steaming! Line the buttered bowl with the pastry.

Mix all the filling ingredients together and pack into the pastry-lined bowl. Roll out the remaining piece of pastry and put on top. Scrunch the edges together to seal. Cut a circle of siliconised paper to go over the top of the pastry and snap on the lid of the pudding bowl. Or tie on a pudding cloth or a piece of foil. Put the bowl into a suciently large saucepan to hold it comfortably, and pour water into the pan to come about half way up the sides of the bowl. Cover the saucepan with a lid, and put on the heat. Bring to a gentle simmer, and cook for $2\frac{1}{2}$ hours, topping up the water from time to time. Serve piping hot, straight from the basin.

Fruit Puddings

Fruit puds can be amongst the least calorific of sweet things, if you take a recipe like Poached Peaches with Blackcurrant Sauce. They can also be deliciously warming, like the mincemeat-stuffed apples served with foamy orange-flavoured sauce, which is one of my favourites. Best of all the fruit-based puddings is the raspberry and lemon one, combining the inimitable flavours of cooked raspberries (different and altogether better than that of uncooked raspberries) and lemon.

Lemon & Raspberry Pudding

This lovely pudding separates whilst cooking to form a very light sponge-like top with a thick raspberry-lemon sauce underneath. I like it best served warm. It doesn't take long to make, once all the ingredients are collected together, and if you have a food processor all except the whisking of the whites can be done in that.

Another wonderful thing about this delicious pud is that it freezes perfectly. I discovered this quite by chance, when I had a whole pud left after dinner in the hotel one evening and, as is my wont with left-overs, I tucked it into the deep freeze for the family to eat up at a later date. It emerged from the freezer for Sunday lunch two or three weeks later. I warmed it up, and I don't think I could have told in any way that it had been frozen.

Serves 8

1½ lb (700 g) raspberries	juice of 2 lemons
3 oz (75 g) butter	6 eggs
8 oz (225 g) caster sugar	2 oz (50 g) flour
grated rind of 3 lemons	½ pint (300 ml) milk

Put the raspberries into an ovenproof dish – I use a large soufflé dish. Put the butter into a bowl and cream it, gradually adding the caster sugar. Beat the butter and sugar together until they are pale and fluffy. Beat in the grated lemon rind then gradually add the lemon juice. Separate the eggs, and beat in the yolks one by one. If the mixture curdles, don't worry, it doesn't affect the end result. Beat in the sieved flour, and lastly the milk.

Whisk the egg whites until stiff and, using a large metal spoon, fold them into the butter and lemon mixture. Pour this on top of the raspberries, and put the dish into a roasting tin. Pour about 2 in (5 cm) hot water into the tin, and put it all into a moderate oven, 350°F (180°C) Gas mark 4 (bottom right-hand oven in a 4-door Aga). Bake for 40–45 minutes until golden and firm on top. Serve warm or cold, whichever you prefer.

Pineapple Meringue Pudding

Of all the misalliances, I am married to a man who doesn't like sweet things. It is truly tragic! However, having said that, Gog really does love about three puddings, one of which is this **Pineapple Meringue Pud**.

Serves 6–8

1½ pints (900 ml) milk	1 medium-sized fresh
4 eggs, separated	pineapple, with the skin
8 oz (225 g) caster sugar	cut off and the fruit cut
1 level tablespoon cornflour	into chunks, or a 1 lb
	(450 g) tin, drained of
	its juice

Heat the milk slowly in a saucepan. In a bowl, beat together the egg yolks, 2 oz (50 g) caster sugar and the cornflour, beating until they are well mixed. When the milk just begins to form a skin in the saucepan, pour a little of it into the yolk mixture, then pour this all back into the pan with the rest of the milk. Stir continuously over a moderate heat, until the sauce just boils. Draw off the heat and stir in the pineapple pieces. Pour this all into a wide, shallow ovenproof dish.

Whisk the egg whites until fairly stiff, then gradually add the remaining caster sugar, little by little, whisking all the time until all the sugar is incorporated. Spoon this over the pineapple custard and bake in a moderate oven, 350°F (180°C) Gas mark 4 (bottom right-hand oven in a 4-door

Aga) for 25–30 minutes, until the top of the meringue is just turning golden brown. Serve warm, with cream for those who like it.

Baked Apples Stuffed with Mincemeat, with Orange Sabayon Sauce

Choose large cooking apples for this, the ideal pud for a cold winter's evening supper party. The contrasting textures of the baked apple, the (preferably homemade) mincemeat, and the orange-flavoured, foamy sabayon are quite delicious.

Serves 6

6 large cooking apples *½ lb (225 g) mincemeat* *(page 122)*	Orange sabayon sauce: *2 eggs* *grated rind of 2 oranges* *2 oz (50 g) caster sugar* *juice of 1 orange*

Wipe the apples, remove their cores and scoop a hole round where the core was, about 1½ in (4 cm) in diameter. I like to make a wide hole in each apple because then you can get more stung in. Put the apples in an ovenproof dish. Score a line round the waist of each apple, to help to prevent it bursting during cooking. Divide the mincemeat between the 6 apples. Cover the apples with 2 butter papers, and bake in a moderate oven, 350°F (180°C) Gas mark 4 (bottom right-hand oven in a 4-door Aga) for about 35–40 minutes, until the apples are soft.

Meanwhile, put the eggs into a bowl, together with the grated orange rind. Put the bowl over a saucepan of gently simmering water and whisk the eggs (this is easiest with a hand-held electric whisk), gradually adding the caster sugar. Whisk until the eggs are almost white and so thick that when you leave a trail in the mixture it holds its shape. Remove the bowl from the heat and carry on whisking, adding the orange juice. It will become a bit thinner, but don't worry; keep on whisking and it will thicken up again. When cooler, leave, and give it a quick whisk again before serving with the warm baked apples. Serve it in a bowl handed round separately.

Poached Peaches with Blackcurrant Sauce

As puddings go, this one isn't too laden with calories. It makes a refreshing finale for a rich dinner during the summer months when peaches are available. I like to leave the peaches whole; halved, stoned peaches seem to shrink when poached, whereas a whole peach on a plate looks much more attractive. You can serve whipped cream with this for those who like it.

Serves 6

---

6 large peaches
4 oz (125 g) granulated
* sugar*
a few strips of pared lemon
* rind*

a vanilla pod, or a few drops
* of vanilla essence*
Blackcurrant sauce:
1 lb (450 g) blackcurrants
3–4 oz (75–125 g) caster
* sugar*

Skin the peaches, dipping them into boiling water for about 10 seconds, so that their skins will slip off easily.

Put 2 pints (1.1 litres) water, the sugar, lemon rind and vanilla (pod or essence) into a fairly small saucepan, so that the syrup is quite deep for cooking the peaches. Heat the water so that the sugar dissolves, then boil rapidly for 5 minutes. Then add the peaches. If it is a small pan, do them in 2 lots, 3 at a time. Poach them for about 10 minutes, turning them over during simmering, using a metal slotted spoon. Remove them to a serving dish, draining them well, and if any juice accumulates in the dish, dab it away with kitchen paper before pouring the blackcurrant sauce over.

Put the blackcurrants and sugar together in a saucepan (don't bother to top and tail the blackcurrants), and over a gentle to moderate heat, cook until the juices begin to run and the sugar dissolves. Draw the pan off the heat, cool, then liquidize in a blender. Taste to see whether it is sweet enough for your liking and add more sugar if you prefer it a bit sweeter. Then sieve the blackcurrant purée over the peaches in the serving dish. Serve cold, with whipped cream and Vanilla Biscuits (page 149).

Tarte aux Fruits

You can vary the fruits you use according to what you can get! The glaze may sound a fiddle but believe me, it is really worth it as it gives the finished tart a most professional appearance.

Serves 6

For the pastry:
3 oz (84 g) butter, hard from the fridge, cut into bits
5 oz (140 g) flour
1 tablespoon icing sugar
½ teaspoon vanilla essence, or a few drops of vanilla extract

For the crème pâtissière:
¾ pint (420 ml) single cream
4 egg yolks – from large eggs
3 oz (84 g) caster sugar
½ teaspoon vanilla essence, or a few drops of vanilla extract
1 level teaspoon cornflour

64

For the fruit and glaze:
A selection of fruit, such as
  halved strawberries,
  sliced peaches or
  nectarines, halved green
  or black grapes, whole
  raspberries, halved
  apricots, etc

*Good apricot jam, warmed
and sieved, to brush over
the entire surface*

Put the ingredients for the pastry into a food processor and whizz till the mixture resembles fine crumbs. Pat this firmly around the sides and base of a 9 in (23 cm) flan dish or a rectangular oven tray measuring approximately 11 × 7½ in (28 × 19 cm).

Put the dish in the fridge for at least one hour, then bake in a moderate oven, 350°F (180°C) Gas mark 4, till the pastry is pale golden brown – if the pastry shows signs of slipping down the sides at all as it cooks, press it back up with the back of a metal spoon. The cooking time will take about 20–25 minutes.

Make the crème pâtissière by beating together all the ingredients well. Cook over a very low temperature in a thick-bottomed pan, stirring all the time till the cream thickens – this takes some time. Alternatively, put the bowl in a microwave oven on a medium heat setting for 2 minutes. Take out, whisk well and repeat three times, giving in total 8 minutes' cooking time. The cream should be thickened beautifully. If you are in any doubt, give it another minute's cooking.

Leave the cream to cool in the bowl, then spoon it over the base of the baked pastry case. Arrange the sliced fruit in circles – this is fun. Brush the entire surface with the sieved apricot jam – I mean even the sides of the pastry.

Jellies & Mousses

These recipes can be delicious variations on seasonal favourites, or you can use frozen fruits for them, adding a touch of summer sparkle to a wintery dinner. A light, creamy-textured mousse rounds off an otherwise rather rich dinner perfectly.

Fresh Orange Jelly

A lot of people still associate jellies with nursery food. Most, and me included, nurture a secret and often unfulfilled passion for them. A proper jelly, made with real fruit juice, makes a perfect pudding to follow a filling main course such as oxtail stew. It is very low in calories, full of vitamin C, and can be served either by itself or with a dish of sliced oranges. If you have a lovely jelly mould, you can turn the jelly out on to an ashet and surround it with the fruit. I must confess that I always have to use two moulds in the shape of rabbits, to which our children are greatly attached; but I feel uneasy at the glee with which they spoon off the rabbits' heads and other parts of their anatomies!

Serves 6–8

---

1 oz (25 g) gelatine
1¾ pints (1 litre) fresh
squeezed orange juice – I
find that 10 good oranges

give just less than this
amount and I make it up
with cold water
2 oz (50 g) caster sugar

Sprinkle the gelatine over ¼ pint (150 ml) cold water then gently warm the gelatine and water until the gelatine has dissolved completely – I find this easier to do in a saucepan. Pour some of the orange juice into the gelatine in the saucepan and stir in the sugar. Heat, stirring, until the sugar has dissolved completely. Strain it through a sieve, mix with the rest of the fresh orange juice, and pour into a bowl or mould. If you are going to use a mould, rinse it out with cold water first to make it easier to turn the jelly out. Leave the jelly in the fridge to set for several hours or overnight.

Mulled Wine & Black Grape Jelly

You can serve this jelly at any time of the year, as a refreshing finale to a rich dinner, but I think it is rather a winter's pud. It is particularly good around Christmas time, when so much of the food we traditionally eat is extremely filling and rich. I love the black grapes in the jelly, because it gives a contrast in texture, something to chew against the smoothness of the jelly. Men particularly seem to love wine jellies, and I must confess that our children yearn for leftovers of this particular one. I am slightly worried by their alcoholic tendencies, but I do so love to see things eaten up that I usually let them indulge!

Serves 6

---

pared rind of 1 orange and
  ½ lemon
2 oz (50 g) caster sugar
6–10 cloves
2 small or 1 large cinnamon
  sticks

just over 1 oz (25 g) gelatine
¾ pint (450 ml) red wine
8 oz (225 g) black grapes,
  cut in half and deseeded

Put ½ pint (300 ml) water into a saucepan together with the orange and lemon rinds, the sugar, cloves and cinnamon and heat until it just reaches boiling point, then draw aside and leave to sit for 2 hours (or overnight) to let the flavours infuse.

Put ¼ pint (150 ml) water into a small saucepan and sprinkle the gelatine over it. Then gently warm this until the gelatine has completely dissolved. Stir the gelatine into the infused water, and strain this into the wine, stirring well. Divide the halved and seeded grapes between 6 glasses holding ¼ pint (150 ml) each, and pour the liquid jelly over them, filling each glass to the brim. As it sets, stir the contents of each glass – carefully so as not to spill – with a teaspoon, to distribute the grapes through the jelly. Decorate each glass with a few extra black grapes, if you like, or just serve as they are.

Fresh Lime Soufflé

Recently, thanks to our obliging wholesale fruit and vegetable suppliers in Portree, we have been able to get fresh limes regularly. So we have been making favourites like lemon soufflé, using limes instead. Limes are close relatives to lemons in the fruit world, but they have their own individual, distinct and pungent fragrance and taste. A soufflé made with limes makes a most subtle, delicious and rather different version of a great favourite.

Serves 6–8

6 limes	½ oz (15 g) gelatine
4 eggs, separated	½ pint (300 ml) double
4 oz (125 g) caster sugar	cream

Grate the rind from the limes into a medium-sized bowl. Add the egg yolks to the same bowl and whisk, using either an electric hand-held whisk, or a rotary whisk (much harder work). Gradually add the caster sugar, whisking all the time, and continue whisking until the mixture is very thick and pale.

Squeeze the juice from the limes, putting the juice from 4 of them into a small saucepan, and pouring the rest of the juice into the yolk mixture, whisking until it is well incorporated. Sprinkle the gelatine on to the juice in the pan, let it soak in for a minute then, over a gentle heat, dissolve the gelatine completely until there is no sign of any grains. Add the gelatine lime juice to the yolk mixture, stirring thoroughly, and leave in a cool place until the mixture thickly coats the back of a spoon. Whip the cream, until it is thick but not stiff, then fold it into the setting lime mixture.

Whisk the egg whites until very stiff and, using a large metal spoon, quickly and thoroughly fold them into the other mixture. Pour the soufflé into a glass or china bowl. I try not to put any gelatine-containing mousse like this into the fridge (unless it is very hot weather) because I find that the gelatine seems to toughen up. A larder is an ideal place to leave it, but failing that put it in the fridge and try to remember to take it out and leave at room temperature for an hour or two before serving.

Crushed Raspberry Mousse

For years I've been making raspberry mousse using liquidised and sieved raspberries. Recently, I thought of cooking the raspberries a bit instead. It was the smell of raspberry jam which put the idea into my head, because it is one of the best of all cooking smells, and the flavour of cooked raspberries is superior by far to the flavour of the fruit uncooked. I don't bother with liquidising and sieving – I just crush the fruit against the sides of the saucepan as it cooks; I like the texture of the bits of raspberry through the mousse.

Serves 6–8

---

1 lb (450 g) raspberries	*1 sachet (½ oz/15 g) gelatine*
4 eggs, separated	*½ pint (300 ml) double*
4 oz (125 g) caster sugar	*cream*

Put the raspberries into a saucepan and over a moderate heat cook them until the juice just begins to run. Crush the raspberries against the sides of the saucepan as much as you can. Remove from the heat and leave until completely cold.

Whisk the egg yolks and gradually whisk in the caster sugar until the mixture is very thick and pale. Using a slotted spoon, scoop the cold, crushed raspberries from the saucepan with as little of their juice as possible and stir them into the yolk and sugar mixture. Sprinkle the gelatine over 6 tablespoons water, in a small saucepan. Heat gently until the granules of gelatine have dissolved. Stir this into the raspberry mixture.

Whip the cream until thick but not stiff and fold it into the raspberry mixture. Leave to set until the mixture thickly coats the back of a spoon. Then whisk the egg whites until stiff and, using a large metal spoon, quickly and thoroughly fold them into the raspberry cream mixture. Pour this into a glass or china bowl and leave to set.

Rhubarb & Ginger Mousse

For anyone who grows rhubarb this is a marvellous dish to make, elevating rhubarb from its more usual position as an everyday fruit to a party pudding. In this recipe I have deliberately left out any sugar when cooking the rhubarb, because for my taste there is enough in the mousse. When you have stirred the rhubarb purée into the yolk and sugar mixture, taste and see if it is sweet enough for your liking; if you think it could do with a bit more sugar, whip 1–2 oz (25–50 g) into the cream, and add it that way.

Serves 6–8

1½ lb (700 g) rhubarb, trimmed and cut into 1 in (2.5 cm) chunks	1 rounded teaspoon ground ginger
1 orange	½ pint (300 ml) double cream
½ oz (15 g) gelatine	8 pieces preserved ginger, drained of their syrup, optional
4 eggs, separated	
8 oz (225 g) caster sugar	

Put the chunks of trimmed rhubarb in a saucepan. Grate the orange rind into a large clean bowl and set aside. Squeeze the orange juice and pour it over the rhubarb in the pan. Cover the saucepan with a lid and cook on a moderate heat until the rhubarb is quite soft, about 20–25 minutes. Draw the pan off the heat and cool, then liquidise the rhubarb to a smooth purée.

Sprinkle the gelatine over 5 tablespoons water in a small saucepan, and put on a gentle heat to warm until the gelatine granules are completely dissolved. Keep warm. Put the egg yolks into the bowl with the grated orange rind and whisk, gradually adding the caster sugar, until the mixture is very thick and pale. Whisk in the ginger. Then fold in the cold rhubarb purée, and stir in the melted warm gelatine.

Whip the cream until thick but not stiff, and fold this into the rhubarb mixture. When the mixture is thick enough with the setting gelatine to thickly coat the back of a spoon, whisk the egg whites until very stiff and, quickly and thoroughly, using a large metal spoon, fold them into the creamy mixture. Pour this into a glass or china bowl. I like to cut pieces of preserved ginger into slivers and arrange them in a circle around the edge of the mousse; but this is optional.

Kirsch & Black Cherry Mousse

I admit that I use tinned black cherries for this recipe. I now feel that I have to go on the defence and say that I don't class tinned black cherries along with other tinned fruit, which on the whole I despise as being an extremely extravagant way of consuming vast quantities of calories in the heavy, sugar-saturated preserving syrup. However, black cherries go well with the Kirsch which flavours this mousse, even though Godfrey groans at the cost! But as it is intended for a special sort of occasion, I feel my conscience can get away with it. The warm Chocolate Sauce (see page 156) makes it a Rolls Royce of puds.

Serves 8

---

*2 15 oz (425 g) tins black
    cherries, stoned
6 eggs, separated
4 oz (125 g) caster sugar
½ oz (15 g) gelatine*

*3 fl oz (75 ml) Kirsch
½ pint (300 ml) double
    cream
Chocolate Sauce (page
    156)*

Drain the juice off the black cherries and put them into a glass or china serving bowl. Put the egg yolks in a large bowl and whisk them, gradually adding the sugar. Whisk until the mixture is very thick and pale. Whisk in the Kirsch.

Put 5 tablespoons of cold water into a small saucepan and sprinkle the gelatine over it. Over a low heat warm this until the grains of gelatine dissolve completely. Whisk this into the Kirsch-flavoured mixture. Whip the cream until thick but not stiff and fold this into the mixture. Leave until the mixture is just set enough to thickly coat the back of a spoon. Then whisk the egg whites until very stiff and, using a large metal spoon, quickly and thoroughly fold them into the Kirsch mixture. Pour over the cherries in the serving bowl, and fold the cherries through the mousse. If they sink to the bottom, it doesn't matter a bit, just remember to tell your guests to dig deep into the bowl if they help themselves to the mousse! Serve with chocolate sauce, warm but not too hot.

Strawberry & Orange Mousse

We first encountered strawberries served with orange juice when we lived in Italy. There was disappointment at first, then as we ate the strawberries we all realized just how much more delicious they were. The sharp citrus flavour brings out the true flavour of strawberries much better than cream does.

Serves 6–8

1 lb (450 g) strawberries, mushy ones are fine for this recipe	*grated rind of 2 oranges, juice of 1*
4 eggs, separated	*½ oz (15 g) gelatine*
5 oz (150 g) caster sugar	*½ pint (300 ml) double cream*

If you have a food processor, put the strawberries into it and whizz, or do the same in a blender, pushing the fruit down towards the blades. Sieve the strawberry purée to remove the seeds. Put the egg yolks in a bowl and whisk, gradually adding the sugar, until the mixture is very thick and pale. Grate the orange rinds into this, and stir in the strawberry purée.

Put 2 tablespoons water into a small saucepan, and add to it the juice of 1 orange. Sprinkle the gelatine over and then heat gently, until the grains of gelatine have dissolved completely. Stir this into the strawberry mixture, and leave until it is thickening. Whip the cream until it is thick but not stiff. Fold the cream into the strawberry mixture and leave until it is thick enough to coat the back of a spoon thickly. Whisk the egg whites until very stiff and, using a large metal spoon, fold them quickly and thoroughly into the mixture. Pour into a glass or china serving bowl and leave to set.

Apricot & Orange Mousse

We are very lucky at Kinloch to be able to get the best dried apricots that I've ever come across. They are plump and delicious enough to eat just as they are, to occasionally quell the craving for something sweet – and to keep my hand from straying towards a much more fattening left-over pudding from the hotel dining-room! In this mousse I use the dried apricots, combining them with orange and brandy to make one of my favourite mousses.

Serves 6–8

---

8 oz (225 g) dried apricots	*½ pint (300 ml) double*
3 eggs, separated	* cream*
2 oranges	*3 fl oz (75 ml) brandy*
3 oz (75 g) caster sugar	*toasted flaked almonds to*
½ oz (15 g) gelatine	* decorate, optional*

Soak the apricots for 30 minutes, then simmer gently for another 30 minutes until they are soft and swollen. Put the egg yolks in a large bowl. Grate the orange rind into the yolks, and squeeze the orange juice into the apricots. Liquidise the apricots together with the orange juice. Whisk the yolks, gradually adding the sugar, and whisking until the mixture is pale and very thick. Fold the apricot purée into this mixture.

Put 4 tablespoons water into a small saucepan and sprinkle the gelatine over it. Heat gently, until the grains of gelatine have dissolved completely. Stir this into the apricot mixture.

Whip the cream until thick, but not stiff. Fold this into the apricot mixture. When this mixture is set enough to coat the back of a spoon thickly, whisk the egg whites until they are very stiff and, using a large metal spoon, fold them quickly and thoroughly into the creamy apricot mixture. Pour this into a glass or china bowl for serving, and decorate, if you like, with toasted flaked almonds sprinkled over the top. Leave to set.

Blackberry & Lemon Suèdoise

A suèdoise is a jellied fruit purée, moulded and turned out. It is often covered with whipped cream, and I like the cream covered with small meringues.

Serves 8

---

2 lb (900 g) blackberries – I make this in the winter using frozen fruit	gelatine
	$\frac{1}{2}$ pint (300 ml) double cream
pared rind and juice of 2 lemons	Vanilla Meringues (page 92), piped $1\frac{1}{2}$ in (4 cm) in diameter
5–6 oz (150–175 g) caster sugar	

Put the blackberries into a saucepan, over a gentle heat, until the juices begin to run; continue cooking until they are soft. As they cook, add to them the pared lemon rind, lemon juice and 4 oz (125 g) caster sugar. Remove the saucepan from the heat, cool, liquidise in a blender and sieve – sieving may sound an unnecessary fiddle after liquidising, but it is worth while because those tiny woody seeds in brambles just don't break down. Measure the purée and take ½ oz (15 g) gelatine to each 1 pint (600 ml) purée; 2 lb (900 g) blackberries generally gives about 2 pints (1.1 litres) purée.

Put ¼ pint (150 ml) water into a small saucepan and sprinkle the gelatine over it, then heat gently until the grains of gelatine dissolve completely. Stir this into the purée, stirring thoroughly to make sure that it is well mixed in. Pour into a bowl to set – rinse the bowl out with cold water first, and put into the fridge for several hours. It sets perfectly well if made in the morning for dinner the same evening.

When the purée is set, fill the sink with very hot water, hold the bowl of purée in it and count to 15. Take it out of the water, hold a flan dish or similar flat serving dish over the bowl, turn it upside down and give a gentle shake. The jellied purée should descend from the bowl on to the serving dish. If it doesn't, carefully turn it the right way up again and put it back in the water for a further count of 10; this should do the trick. Don't do what I once did, which was to absent-mindedly plunge the whole bowl into the water so that the surface of the jellied purée was awash.

Whip the cream, sweeten it with 1–2 oz (25–50 g) sugar if you like – this suèdoise is not sweet – spread the cream over the purée and cover the cream with tiny meringues.

Gooseberry & Elderflower Suèdoise

I only make gooseberry suèdoise when elderflowers are in season, because somehow it is so ordinary without the exquisite elderflower flavour. I have tried to freeze elder-flowers, but they became tasteless, sadly.

1½ lb (700 g) gooseberries
6 oz (175 g) caster sugar
4 good handfuls elderflowers
gelatine

½ pint (300 ml) double
 cream
Vanilla Meringues (page
 92), piped 1½ in (4 cm)
 in diameter

Don't bother to top and tail the gooseberries, they are going to be liquidised and sieved, so it isn't necessary. Put the gooseberries into a saucepan, together with 1 pint (600 ml) water, the caster sugar, and the elderflowers. Cover with a lid and gently simmer for 30 minutes, then remove from the heat and leave to go completely cold. This gives maximum infusion for the elderflowers. Fish out the elderflowers, and liquidise the rest in a blender. Then sieve, to get a really smooth purée. Measure the purée and take ½ oz (15 g) gelatine for every 1 pint (600 ml) purée.

Put ¼ pint (150 ml) water into a small saucepan, and sprinkle the gelatine over it, then heat gently, until the grains of gelatine have dissolved. Stir this through the gooseberry purée. Rinse out a bowl with cold water, pour the purée into the wetted bowl and put into the fridge to set. If made in the morning, it will be set for dinner that same evening. When the purée is set, fill the sink with very hot water, and dip the bowl into the water for a count of 15. Then remove the bowl from the water, hold a flat serving dish over it (I like to use a flan dish), turn the bowl upside down, and give a gentle shake. If the jellied purée doesn't descend from bowl to plate, carefully turn it the right way up and put it back in the hot water; count to 10, and repeat the performance.

Whip the cream until stiff and, using a palette knife, cover the jelly with the cream. Cover the cream with tiny meringues.

Meringues

I love meringues, which will surprise no one who knows me! They are extremely versatile, and in some form they feature on the menu at Kinloch every week.

I used to suffer terribly from meringues sticking to the paper after they were cooked, but siliconised paper puts an end to that problem. The other necessities for meringue-making are an entirely clean bowl and whisk, be it a hand whisk or an electric one, and caution in separating the egg yolks from the whites; the tiniest speck of yolk will prevent the whites from whisking up into stiff peaks. If you do get a speck of yolk in the whites (and it uncannily and invariably seems to happen with the sixth or seventh white) you can usually manage to fish it out with half an egg shell. If you do this, make sure it is in a good light so that you can see if there is any trace of yolk streaking the whites.

Meringues look most decorative sandwiched together with generous amounts of whipped cream and piled on an ashet (that is what we call a large flat serving plate in Scotland). If there is a sauce to be served with them hand it round separately in a sauce boat, jug or bowl.

Ginger Meringues with Orange & Ginger Cream

Like most meringues, these can be made several days ahead, and stored in an air-tight tin.

Serves 6

---

4 egg whites
8 oz (225 g) caster sugar
1 rounded dessertspoon
  ground ginger
½ pint (300 ml) double
  cream

grated rind of 2 oranges
6 pieces of preserved ginger,
  drained from the syrup
  and cut in slivers

Put a piece of siliconised paper on a baking sheet.

In a bowl, whisk the egg whites until fairly stiff and beginning to form peaks, then, whisking continuously, gradually add the caster sugar until it is all incorporated. Sieve the ground ginger on to the mixture and, using a metal spoon, quickly and carefully fold the ginger in. Using a piping bag with a large nozzle, pipe the meringue mixture in even 2½ in (6 cm) rounds on to the paper, and bake for about 3 hours approximately, in a low oven, 250°F (130°C) Gas mark 1 (top left-hand oven of a 4-door Aga). Then remove from the oven, pick the meringues off the paper and cool them on a wire rack.

Whip the cream, together with the finely grated orange rind, until the cream is stiff enough to sandwich the meringues together. When it is stiff, gently fold in the slivers of ginger, then divide the cream between the meringue halves. Serve the whole meringues piled up on a small ashet. If you like, a dish of sliced oranges, with all the pith removed, goes well with these gingery meringues.

Chocolate Meringues with Brandy Flavoured Cream

Cooking the egg whites a little over a saucepan of simmering water whilst they are being whisked gives an extremely thick meringue mixture. This quantity gives 12 meringue halves, each about 2½ in (6 cm) in diameter, so there are 6 meringues when sandwiched together with the whipped cream.

Serves 6

---

4 egg whites
8 oz (225 g) icing sugar, sieved
1 oz (25 g) cocoa powder
½ pint (300 ml) double cream
3 tablespoons brandy

1 rounded dessertspoon caster sugar (optional, it depends if you like the cream slightly sweetened, which I do, or feel that there is enough sweetness from the meringues)

Put the egg whites and the sieved icing sugar in a bowl and put the bowl over a saucepan of gently simmering water. Whisk them together until the mixture is really thick – this takes about 5 minutes. Remove the bowl from the heat, and continue whisking for a further couple of minutes. This whisking is quite effortless if you use an electric whisk; if you use a rotary hand whisk it does become rather hard work as the mixture thickens.

Sieve the cocoa powder over the meringue and fold it in as thoroughly as possible, so that there are no hidden pockets of cocoa lurking in the meringue.

Put a piece of siliconised paper on a baking sheet, putting a dab of meringue mixture at each corner under the paper to hold it down flat. Then pipe 12 mounds, each about 2½ in (6 cm) in diameter, on the paper. I like to use a large fluted nozzle, which makes the end result rather more

83

decorative than if a plain nozzle is used. Bake them in a low oven, 225°F (110°C) Gas mark ¼ (top left-hand oven in a 4-door Aga) for about 3 hours. Remove from the oven, pick them off the paper and cool them on a rack.

Meanwhile whip the cream together with the brandy and sugar, until it is really stiff. Divide it between the meringues, sandwiching them together.

Crunchy Brown Sugar Meringues with Rhubarb & Ginger Sauce

These meringues tend not to keep as well as those made with white sugar only, so I make them the day I plan to serve them.

Serves 6

---

4 egg whites	½ pint (300 ml) double
4 oz (125 g) granulated	cream
sugar	Rhubarb and Ginger Sauce
4 oz (125 g) demerara sugar	(page 158)

Put a piece of siliconised paper on a baking sheet.

Whisk the egg whites until fairly stiff and beginning to stand in peaks. Then, still whisking continuously, add the sugars a spoonful at a time until they are all incorporated into the meringue and the mixture is really stiff. Pipe into 12 even mounds about 2½ in (6 cm) in diameter, on to the paper. Put the meringues into a moderate oven, 350°F (180°C) Gas mark 4 (bottom right-hand oven in a 4-door Aga) for 3–5 minutes (no longer) then turn the heat down to about 250°F (130°C) Gas mark 1 (or move them to the top left-hand oven in the Aga), and bake for 2½–3 hours. Remove from the paper and cool them on a rack.

Whip the cream until stiff and sandwich the cooled

meringue halves together. Serve with Rhubarb and Ginger Sauce handed separately in a bowl or sauce boat.

Pavlova

How I do love pavlovas – they have a marshmallow-like texture and a pronounced vanilla flavour which is everything my sweet tooth craves. A pavlova doesn't take a second to make; I timed it once and, having got out all the ingredients, it took me 5 minutes to put them together and get the pavlova into the oven.

The best fruit to cover a pavlova is rather a sharp fruit such as raspberries, pineapple, or blackcurrants which have been gently stewed. Drain the fruit of any juice, fold into whipped cream and spread it on top of the cooked pavlova.

Pavlova is an excellent pudding for a large party, for any age group. The only person I've come across who doesn't love a pavlova is Meriel, our small daughter, who hates all meringues and doesn't much like puddings at all. How I wish I was the same!

Serves 6–8

---

4 egg whites	*1 teaspoon wine vinegar*
8 oz (225 g) caster sugar	*1 rounded teaspoon cornflour*
1 teaspoon vanilla essence	*a pinch of cream of tartar*

Line a baking sheet with a piece of siliconised paper. Put the egg whites into a large bowl and whisk until stiff. Continue whisking, adding the caster sugar gradually, until all the sugar is incorporated and the meringue is stiff. Measure on to the meringue mixture the vanilla essence and wine vinegar; sieve the cornflour and cream of tartar over the meringue and fold them all quickly together.

Spread the mixture on to the paper-lined baking sheet, and bake in a moderate oven, 350°F (180°C) Gas mark 4 (bottom right-hand oven in a 4-door Aga) for 5 minutes then reduce the heat to 250°F (130°C) Gas mark 1 (or move the baking sheet to the top left-hand oven of the Aga) and bake for a further 1¼ hours, or thereabouts. Remove from the oven, cool, then turn upside down on to a large serving dish – if you haven't one large enough, a pretty tray does as a good substitute – and cover the surface with whipped cream and the fruit of your choice, or a combination of fruit; for example, raspberries and chopped pineapple go together extremely well. I reckon ½ pint (300 ml) double cream to a pavlova of this size.

Gâteau Diane

This gooey concoction of rich chocolate butter cream and meringue is right up my street. It is an elaborate and delicious pudding, a calorific disaster but worth every mouthful.

Serves about 10

---

4 egg whites
8 oz (225 g) caster sugar
1 level tablespoon instant coffee powder – powder, as opposed to granules
Buttercream filling:
8 oz (225 g) butter, unsalted if possible
6 oz (175 g) icing sugar

3 egg yolks
4 oz (125 g) plain chocolate
1 tablespoon strong black coffee
2 rounded tablespoons grated chocolate to decorate, or 1 tablespoon sieved icing sugar

---

Put a sheet of siliconised paper on a baking sheet and draw on it 2 circles, about 7–8 in (18–20 cm) in diameter. Whisk the egg whites until fairly stiff, then gradually whisk in all the caster sugar, until it is all incorporated and the meringue is very stiff. Fold in the coffee powder, divide the mixture between the pencilled circles, smooth them round and bake for 3 hours in a low oven, 225°F (110°C) Gas mark ¼ (top left-hand oven in a 4-door Aga). Then remove from the oven, carefully lift off the paper and cool on a wire rack.

Meanwhile make the buttercream. Beat the butter until pale and creamy, then add the sieved icing sugar, beating until the mixture is fluffy. Beat in the egg yolks one by one, beating well between each one. Put the chocolate and coffee together in a small bowl over a saucepan of gently simmering water, stir until it melts to a thick cream, cool, then beat into the butter mixture.

Spread some of this buttercream on one layer of the meringue, put the other layer on top, then spread the remaining buttercream over the top – and the sides too, if you wish. Decorate either by sprinkling the grated chocolate over the top, or by sieving icing sugar over the surface instead.

This rich meringue gâteau is even more delicious if made a day or two in advance.

Crunchy Almond Meringue Cake

Serves 6–8

4 oz (125 g) dried apricots	*1 oz (25 g) flaked almonds*
2 strips of lemon rind	*½ pint (300 ml) double*
4 egg whites	*cream, whipped*
6 oz (175 g) caster sugar	*1 rounded dessertspoon icing*
2 oz (50 g) ground almonds	*sugar*

Put the dried apricots into a small saucepan with 1 pint

(600 ml) water and the lemon rind. By using a potato peeler to pare the rind from the lemon, I find that I avoid including any of the white, bitter pith. Put the saucepan on a gentle heat and simmer for 30 minutes. Drain the apricots.

Line a baking sheet with a piece of siliconised paper and draw on it 2 circles about 7 in (18 cm) in diameter. Put the egg whites into a large bowl and whisk until stiff, then, whisking all the time, add the caster sugar a spoonful at a time until it is all incorporated and the meringue is very stiff. Sieve the ground almonds on to the meringue, sprinkle on the flaked almonds and, using a metal spoon, quickly and gently fold both into the mixture. Divide the meringue between the pencilled circles and smooth into even rounds. Bake in a moderate oven, 350°F (180°C) Gas mark 4 (bottom right-hand oven of a 4-door Aga) for 5 minutes then turn the heat down to 225°F (110°C) Gas mark $\frac{1}{4}$ (or move the meringue rounds into the top left-hand oven of the Aga). Bake for a further 2 hours and 20–30 minutes. Remove from the oven, carefully lift the meringue rounds off the paper and put them on a wire rack to cool.

Meanwhile, snip the cooled, plumped-up apricots into small bits. Mix them into the whipped cream. Spread this over one of the meringue rounds, on a serving dish. Put the remaining round on top and sieve a spoonful of icing sugar over the top for decoration. It makes a lovely thick filling – if you prefer, divide the apricot cream and put half in the middle to sandwich the rounds together, and the rest on top.

It can be rather tricky cutting meringue cakes without getting into a mess. I find that a serrated knife with a sharp point is the answer – stick the point into the middle of the cake and cut with a sawing motion.

Strawberry Cream Meringue Cake with Coffee Icing

Coffee is an unexpectedly enhancing flavour combination with strawberries. This meringue cake makes a few strawberries stretch into a party type of pudding.

Serves 6–8

---

4 egg whites
8 oz (225 g) icing sugar
8 oz (225 g) firm
strawberries
½ pint (300 ml) double
cream, whipped

6 rounded tablespoons sieved
icing sugar
1 level tablespoon instant
coffee powder or granules,
dissolved in 2 tablespoons
hot water

Put a piece of siliconised paper on to a baking sheet and pencil 2 circles on the paper, about 7 in (18 cm) in diameter. Put the egg whites into a large bowl, put the bowl over a saucepan of gently simmering water and sieve the icing sugar into the whites. Whisk – this is easy using an electric hand-held whisk, rather harder work using a rotary whisk as the mixture thickens – until the mixture is really stiff. This takes about 5 minutes. Remove the bowl from on top of the saucepan, whisk for another minute or so, then divide the meringue between the 2 pencilled circles and smooth into rounds. Bake in a low oven, 225°F (110°C) Gas mark ¼ (top left-hand oven of a 4-door Aga) for 2½–3 hours. Remove from the oven, gently and carefully lift off the paper and cool on a wire rack.

Hull the strawberries and cut them into even-sized bits, halving the smaller berries and cutting the larger ones into quarters. Fold them into the stiffly whipped cream and spread this on one of the meringue rounds on a serving plate. Put the remaining round on top. Mix the sieved icing sugar with the coffee and water. Add a drop more water if you find it too stiff and spread the coffee icing over the surface of the meringue. If you like, reserve a few whole strawberries and put them, evenly spaced, round the edge.

Orange Meringue Bombe with Hot Chocolate Sauce

This pudding always goes down well when it features on the menu at Kinloch. It is easy to make, and a real convenience pudding because it has to be made in advance. It can be dug into straight from the deep freeze, because it has a slug of orange liqueur in the mixture that prevents it freezing rock hard.

Serves 6–8

4 egg whites	*grated rind of 2 oranges*
8 oz (225 g) caster sugar	*2 tablespoons orange liqueur*
½ pint (300 ml) double	*Chocolate Sauce (page*
cream	*156)*

Put a piece of siliconised paper on a baking sheet. Put the egg whites into a bowl, and whisk them until stiff. Then, whisking all the time, add the caster sugar spoonful by spoonful until all the sugar is incorporated and the meringue is really stiff. Spoon into even-sized dollops on the paper, and bake in a low oven, 225°F (110°C) Gas mark ¼ (top left-hand oven of a 4-door Aga) for 2½–3 hours. Then remove from the oven, pick the meringues off the paper and cool them on a wire rack.

Meanwhile, whip the cream until stiff. Whip in the orange liqueur (it doesn't matter what you use, Cointreau, Curaçao, Aurum, or any other orange liqueur) and stir in the grated orange rind. Crush the cooled meringues into fairly small bits, but not into powder, and stir them into the cream. At first you will think you have far too much meringue for the amount of cream, but as you fold it together, it mixes well, and there is just the right amount of cream to bind together the crushed meringues. Put the mixture into a polythene tub, cover it and freeze. Serve with a little chocolate sauce poured over each portion.

Ginger Meringue Bombe

A variation on the theme of the orange meringue bombe. Use exactly the same ingredients as for the Orange Meringue Bombe but leave out the orange rind and substitute brandy for the orange liqueur; add 10–12 small pieces of preserved ginger, well drained of their syrup and cut into slivers. Stir the ginger slivers into the cream, meringue and brandy mixture before freezing.

Vanilla Meringues with Raspberry & Cinnamon Sauce

When there are lots of raspberries available these vanilla-flavoured meringues both taste delicious and look stunning served with the jewel-coloured, cinnamon-flavoured sauce.

Serves 6

---

4 egg whites
8 oz (225 g) icing sugar,
  sieved
½ teaspoon vanilla essence

½ pint (300 ml) double
  cream, stiffly whipped
Raspberry and Cinnamon
Sauce (page 162)

Line a baking sheet with a piece of siliconised paper. Put the egg whites into a large bowl with the sieved icing sugar. Put the bowl on top of a saucepan containing simmering water, on a moderate heat, and whisk until the meringue is really thick. This takes about 5 minutes. Remove the bowl from the heat and continue whisking for a minute. Measure the vanilla essence on to the meringue and quickly and carefully fold it in.

Using a piping bag with a wide, fluted nozzle, pipe the meringue mixture onto the prepared baking sheet in 12 even-sized rounds about 2½ in (6 cm) in diameter. Bake in a low oven, 225°F (110°C) Gas mark ¼ (top left-hand oven of a 4-door Aga) for about 2½ hours. Then remove the baking sheet from the oven, pick the meringues off the paper and cool them on a wire rack. When quite cold, sandwich them together with the whipped cream, and pile them on to a serving dish. Serve the sauce separately in a small glass bowl or jug.

Everlasting Favourites

There are some puddings which can't be categorised, and those are the ones in this chapter. Some of them are real traditionals, like Baked Rice Pudding and Queen of Puddings, but they never lose their popularity. Crème Brûlée is my particular favourite, providing it is vanilla-ey enough. It must be the richest of all puddings, too, but oh, so delicious.

Crème Brûlée

My favourite of all puddings – and my father's too. It must
be the richest and most extravagant of all but it is worth
every single calorie. I make this on my birthday, a time for
self-indulgence. When we have it on the menu in the hotel
I always hope I have the will-power not to touch any that
happens to be left over, but I always do! Tastes vary, with
regard to the sugar used for the top of this dream pud, but
personally I prefer caster sugar – I find demerara gives too
obtrusive a flavour, and anything which might mask the
subtle flavour of vanilla is a sacrilege.

Serves 6

---

*1 pint (600 ml) double
    cream
a vanilla pod or a few drops
    of vanilla essence*

*6 egg yolks
1 rounded tablespoon caster
    sugar
more caster sugar for the top*

Put the cream into a very thick-bottomed saucepan, or a
double boiler, and put the vanilla pod into the cream. Heat
until it begins to form a skin. Meanwhile, beat the egg yolks
and the tablespoon of sugar together, then pour the
scalded cream on to the egg yolks, and beat well. Return to
the saucepan. Over a very gentle heat, cook, stirring all the
time, until the cream coats the back of the wooden spoon.
This takes quite a time, about 7–10 minutes, but it can't be
hurried. If the heat is turned up the eggs will curdle, and
that is tragic, enough to make me weep! So be patient, it
will thicken, and when it does coat the back of the spoon,
pour it through a sieve into a shallow ovenproof dish.

Leave it in a cool place for several hours (or overnight).
A skin will form on top. Sprinkle caster sugar over the
surface, not very deep but enough to give an even white
covering. Preheat a grill to red-hot and put the dish under

it. Watch it carefully as the sugar dissolves. When it is just golden and liquid, remove from the heat and leave in a cool place until you are ready to eat it. The sugar will harden and form a glass-like surface which has to be cracked with the back of a spoon.

Queen of Puddings

Dishes go in and out of fashion, and this recipe is one which not many people seem to bother about these days. I think it is high time it came back into fashion again!

Serves 6

---

1 pint (600 ml) milk	*3 oz (75 g) fresh white*
rind of 1 lemon, pared with	*breadcrumbs*
a potato peeler	*3 eggs*
1 oz (25 g) butter	*4 tablespoons raspberry jam*
5 oz (150 g) caster sugar	

Put the milk into a saucepan with the pared lemon rind and heat until the milk is just beginning to form a skin. Remove the saucepan from the heat and stir into it the butter and 2 oz (50 g) of the caster sugar. Fish out the lemon rind and stir until the sugar has dissolved and the butter melted. Then stir in the breadcrumbs and leave it to sit for half an hour.

Separate the eggs and beat the yolks into the milk and breadcrumb mixture. Pour this into a buttered ovenproof dish. Put in a roasting tin with water half way up the sides of the dish, and bake in a low to moderate oven, 325°F (170°C) Gas mark 3 (bottom of the bottom right-hand oven of a 4-door Aga) for 45–50 minutes. Remove from the oven and cool. Spread the jam over the surface.

Whisk the egg whites until stiff, then gradually add the

remaining caster sugar whisking all the time. When the meringue is very stiff, spoon it over the jam, covering it completely, and bake in the oven, at the same temperature, for 30 minutes, until the meringue is pale golden. Serve with cream for those who like it.

Proper Trifle

I always associate trifle with Christmas time, it is traditionally a Christmas dish in our family. The essentials of a proper trifle are a vanilla-flavoured freshly made sponge base, an egg custard, lightly flavoured with vanilla, and not-very-stiffly-whipped cream on top. It doesn't need any decoration, but a few toasted almonds strewn over the cream provide a nice contrast in texture.

Serves 8

---

1 pint (600 ml) milk
4 egg yolks
1 rounded teaspoon cornflour
2 tablespoons caster sugar
a few drops vanilla essence
1 lb (450 g) strawberry jam, preferably home-made
1 wineglass medium-sweet sherry

3 bananas
½ pint (300 ml) double cream, whipped, but not very stiffly
Sponge cake:
2 eggs
2 oz (50 g) caster sugar
a few drops of vanilla essence
2 oz (50 g) plain flour

Make the sponge cake first. Break the eggs into a bowl and beat or whisk until they are just beginning to thicken, then whisk in the caster sugar and vanilla essence and whisk until the mixture holds its shape. Sieve the flour into a bowl, then sieve it again into the egg mixture and, using a metal spoon, fold it in as quickly and thoroughly as possible. Pour this into a greased and lined 8-in (20.5-cm) sandwich tin and bake in a moderate oven, 350°F (180°C) Gas mark 4 (bottom right-hand oven in a 4-door Aga) for 15–20 minutes, until the cake is just beginning to come away from the sides of the tin. Cool it on a wire rack.

Heat the milk in a saucepan until it is just beginning to form a skin. Beat the egg yolks, cornflour, caster sugar and vanilla essence together and pour some of the hot milk on to the mixture. Mix well, then pour it all back into the saucepan with the rest of the hot milk. Over a gentle heat, stir until the custard coats the back of the wooden spoon, thickly enough so that when you run your finger down the back of the spoon through the custard coating it leaves a discernible path. Don't let the custard boil or it will curdle. If it should look as if it is going to curdle, pour it at once into a bowl and whisk with a rotary whisk; but unless the heat is too high under the saucepan it won't curdle, the cornflour helps to prevent this. Cool the custard.

To assemble the trifle put the sponge cake in the bottom of a wide and fairly shallow bowl. Cover it with the strawberry jam. Sprinkle the glass of sherry as evenly as possible over the cake. Peel and slice the bananas and spread them over the cake. Pour the cooled custard over, and cover this with the whipped cream. Keep in a cool place until time to serve.

Baked Rice Pudding

It may seem a bit strange to include a recipe for rice pudding in this book, but I know I am far from being unique in my love of it. A proper baked rice pudding, and I say baked because making it in a saucepan on top of the cooker does us all out of the lovely skin which forms on top, is simple to make and it's good for you. It is one of the few puddings which I like to eat with cream.

Serves 4

---

1 pint (600 ml) milk
2 oz (50 g) pudding rice
*   (not long grain)*
1 oz (25 g) butter

2 level tablespoons caster
*   sugar*
vanilla essence, optional

Butter an ovenproof dish, and pour in the milk. Add the rice, butter and caster sugar, and a few drops of vanilla essence if you like. Put the dish in a low to moderate oven, 325°F (170°C) Gas mark 3 (bottom of the bottom right-hand oven of a 4-door Aga). After about 15 minutes, open the oven and fork the rice through the milk. Repeat this in another 15–20 minutes. Then lower the heat to about 300°F (150°C) Gas mark 2 and cook for a further 2–2½ hours. Serve with cream.

Caramel & Vanilla Custard Cream

This is the Kinloch version of caramel custard, or crème caramel. By using nearly all egg yolks we make the texture far creamier – the more whites you include the more solid is the baked custard. We don't turn ours out, we just cover it with whipped cream and sprinkle a few bits of caramel over the cream.

6 oz (175 g) granulated sugar	2 eggs
	5 egg yolks
1½ pints (900 ml) milk – or better still 1 pint (600 ml) milk and ½ pint (300 ml) single cream	1 rounded tablespoon caster sugar
	about ⅓ pint (200 ml) double cream, whipped, but not very stiffly
2 vanilla pods, or a few drops of vanilla essence	

Put the granulated sugar in a saucepan over a moderate heat. As it begins to dissolve, shake the pan a bit; when it is dissolved and golden brown (watch that it doesn't burn) pour a little of the caramel on to a well-greased tin plate and pour the rest into a warmed, shallow ovenproof dish. Immediately tip and tilt the dish so that the caramel runs as evenly as possible over the base of the dish. Take care not to burn yourself. Set the dish and tin plate aside.

Put the milk into a saucepan with the vanilla pods and heat until a skin is just beginning to form. In a bowl, beat the eggs and egg yolks together with the spoonful of caster sugar – add the vanilla essence at this stage if you are not using pods. Pour a little of the hot milk into the egg mixture, mix well, then pour the rest of the hot milk in, mixing well. Pour the custard into the ovenproof dish.

Carefully put the dish in a large roasting tin and pour water into the tin to come half way up the side of the dish. Put carefully into a low to moderate oven, 325°F (170°C) Gas mark 3 (bottom of the bottom right-hand oven in a 4-door Aga). Bake for 30 minutes, then see if the custard is just set; it will probably need another 15 minutes. When the custard is just set, remove it from the oven. Cool the custard and cover with the whipped cream. Put a piece of greaseproof paper over the caramel on the tin plate and bash it; sprinkle the caramel chips over the cream.

Profiteroles

Piled up in a pyramid, filled with whipped cream and dusted with icing sugar, these look as good as they taste. Hand a rich, dark chocolate sauce separately.

Serves 8

3 oz (75 g) butter	*3 large eggs*
4 oz (125 g) plain flour	*¼–½ pint (150–300 ml) water*

Put the butter, cut in bits, into a saucepan together with between ¼ and ½ pint (150–300 ml) water, and put the pan over a medium heat. As the water in the saucepan heats, the butter will melt into it; don't let it boil.

Sieve the flour on to a piece of paper, or into a bowl. When the butter has completely melted, just let the water and butter come to the boil then immediately take the pan off the heat. Put all the sieved flour into the pan and beat hard, until the paste that forms comes away from the sides of the saucepan. Cool for 20 minutes.

Then beat in the eggs, one at a time, beating really well. The mixture will be glossy.

Rinse a baking tray under the tap, so that it is wet all over. Fill a piping bag with the choux paste and pipe out even-sized rounds – about 1½ in (4 cm) in size. Bake in a hot oven, 425°F (220°C) Gas mark 7 (bottom of the top right-hand oven of a 4-door Aga) for 15–20 minutes. Look at them, then slit each profiterole with the point of a sharp knife to let the steam out of them as they cook. They should be hard to the touch; if they are soft they will collapse as they cool. When they are cooked, cool them on a wire rack. Fill them with sweetened whipped cream, which I like to flavour with grated orange rind. Pile them on a serving dish, dust with sieved icing sugar. Serve with hot Chocolate Sauce (page 156).

Cream & Yoghurt Pudding with Demerara Sugar

This is so easy it's unbelievable. My mother first introduced me to it two or three years ago, and it has become much in demand. It is good served on its own, but also makes a delicious accompaniment to stewed fruit or fresh fruit salad.

Serves 6–8

½ pint (300 ml) double cream

¼ pint (150 ml) natural yoghurt
demerara sugar

Whip the cream fairly stiffly and then stir in the yoghurt. Pour this into a bowl and cover the top with a layer of demerara sugar – as thick or as thin as you like. Leave for several hours or, better still, overnight.

Atholl Brose

This is a rich and alcoholic pud, but a convenient one too, because it has to be made ahead. In fact, I think that the longer it is left, the more pronounced becomes the flavour of the whisky.

Serves 6

---

1 pint (600 ml) double cream
5–6 tablespoons whisky
runny honey to taste

2 oz (50 g) oatmeal (you can't substitute porridge oats for this!)

Put the cream in a bowl and whip until it is fairly thick, then add the whisky, a little at a time, whipping until it is thick enough to hold its shape. Add some honey, a couple of spoonfuls to start with, taste, and add more if you like it sweeter.

Put the oatmeal in a saucepan over a moderate heat and cook it, shaking the pan a little, for 5 minutes. Remove from the heat and cool. Stir the cold toasted oatmeal into the whisky and honey cream, and divide between 6 glasses. Keep in a cool place for several hours, or overnight.

Brandy Snap Pudding

I love the contrasting textures in this – the crisp and crunchy brandy snap layers against the cream and peaches filling. I make the brandy snap layers in the morning for dinner that evening, and assemble it in the early evening.

Serves 6

4 oz (125 g) butter	1 rounded teaspoon ground ginger
4 oz (125 g) caster sugar	
4 tablespoons golden syrup – dip the spoon into a jug of very hot water before spooning the syrup and in between each spoonful	2 tablespoons finely chopped almonds
	grated rind of 1 lemon
	Filling:
4 oz (125 g) plain flour	6 peaches
	½ pint (300 ml) double cream, whipped fairly stiffly

Put the butter, sugar and golden syrup into a saucepan over a medium heat to melt the butter and dissolve the sugar. Remove from the heat, and stir in the sieved flour and ginger, the finely chopped almonds and lemon rind.

Cook it in 2 lots – unless you have 4 baking trays. Cover each baking tray with a piece of siliconised paper. Divide the mixture between the 4 trays, spooning it into circles about $\frac{1}{8}$ in (5 mm) thick. As the mixture cooks it will spread. Bake in a moderate oven, 350°F (180°C) Gas mark 4 (middle of the bottom right-hand oven of a 4-door Aga) for about 10–15 minutes, until the mixture is bubbling and golden. Remove from the oven, neaten the edges so that the circles are tidy, and leave to cool on the tins.

Dip the peaches into boiling water, and the skins will slip off them easily. Slice them and chop them, and stir them into the whipped cream. Put a layer of the brandy snaps on to a serving dish, and spoon some of the peaches and cream evenly over it. Put another layer on top, and repeat the layering until the peaches and cream are all used up; end with a brandy snap layer on top. Don't assemble it much more than an hour before dinner. Cut it like a cake; it is slightly messy, but good.

Chocolate Cream Bavarois

This is a rich and creamy 'set' pudding, quite delicious, and there is never any left over!

Serves 6

---

4 oz (125 g) plain chocolate	1 level dessertspoon cocoa
$\frac{1}{2}$ pint (300 ml) milk	powder
4 egg yolks	$\frac{1}{2}$ oz (15 g) gelatine
4 oz (125 g) caster sugar	$\frac{1}{2}$ pint (300 ml) double
1 rounded teaspoon instant	cream, whipped but not
coffee powder	stiffly
	chocolate for decoration

Break the chocolate into bits and put it in the milk, in a

saucepan. Heat gently until the chocolate has melted.

Put the egg yolks, caster sugar, coffee powder and cocoa in a bowl and beat well together. Pour a little of the chocolatey milk on to the yolk mixture, mix well, and pour back into the saucepan with the rest of the milk. Cook over a gentle heat, stirring all the time, until the custard coats the back of the wooden spoon – this takes about 10 minutes, but don't be tempted to hurry it, because then it will curdle. Remove from the heat.

Sprinkle the gelatine over 4 tablespoons of cold water, let it soak for a minute, then stir it into the hot custard, stirring well as the gelatine dissolves in the heat. Leave the custard to cool, and when it is quite cold fold the whipped cream into it. Pour it into a glass or china serving dish. Decorate, if you like, with chocolate shaved from a block with a potato peeler – I find this the easiest way of getting curly chocolate shavings.

Steamed Ginger & Fig Pudding

In spite of us all perpetually counting calories, deep down people crave the comfort of puddings like this. That is my theory anyway, borne out by the speed with which a steamed pudding is eaten when I make one. I always use a 3-pint (1.7-litre) plastic bowl for steaming, because mine has a natty snap-on lid, which in its turn has a natty snap-on handle; this makes it easy to lift the pudding out of the saucepan of hot water at the end of the cooking time.

Serves 6–8

---

4 oz (125 g) butter
4 oz (125 g) caster sugar
2 eggs
4 oz (125 g) self-raising
  flour

1 heaped teaspoon ground
  ginger
3 oz (75 g) dried figs, cut
  into bits

Butter the cooking bowl well. In another bowl cream together the butter and sugar. When it is really pale and fluffy, beat in the eggs one by one. Sieve the flour and ginger on to the mixture, and fold this in, then fold in the chopped figs. Spoon the mixture into the buttered bowl, cut a circle of siliconised paper to go over the top of the pudding and snap on the lid. Or tie on a pudding cloth or a piece of foil. Put the bowl in a sufficiently large saucepan to hold the bowl comfortably. Pour water into the pan, to come about half way up the side of the bowl, cover the pan with a lid, and simmer gently for 2½ hours, topping up the pan with water from time to time.

This pud is sensational if served with Brandy and Orange Butter (page 156)!

Jams, Chutneys & Sweets

Everything in this chapter would make a lovely present. I personally love to be given a pot of home-made jam, and I know I'm not alone in my appreciation of such gifts. It is so much nicer to get something home-made than yet another box of mass-produced chocolate mints!

Mustard is easy to make, and is an unusual present – and the same goes for a pot of Cumberland jelly, which is especially valued at Christmas time because it is so good with cold turkey, or ham. It is equally good with hot ham, roast lamb or venison. I love other people's chutneys, so to encourage them I give away pots of my own, hoping we can swap flavours.

The fudges and other sweets can be put on little polystyrene trays and wrapped with pretty ribbon to make a really attractive present – I save the small trays that hold 4 apples or tomatoes for this very thing. Alexandra, our eldest daughter, makes very good fudge and chocolate peppermint creams (Isabella makes those too) and as I like our children to put a bit of thought into their present giving, it is worth encouraging them.

Lemon & Elderflower Curd

Lemon curd is delicious, but with elderflowers added to it, the flavour becomes truly special, a real treat.

Makes about 1½ lb (700 g)

2 handfuls of elderflowers	*3 eggs, 1 egg yolk, beaten*
4 oz (125 g) butter	*and strained*
8 oz (225 g) granulated	*finely grated rinds and juice*
sugar	*of 3 lemons*

Carefully strip the tiny elderflowers off their stems into a bowl. Try not to let too many stalks in with them. Put all the other ingredients into the bowl, and put the bowl over a saucepan of boiling water. Stir the contents of the bowl continuously until it thickens – so that it coats the back of the wooden stirring spoon, and when you run your finger down the back of the spoon it makes a distinct mark. Remove from the heat and pour into warmed jars. Cool, cover with waxed paper discs and seal with cellophane jam pot covers. I store lemon curd in the fridge.

You can make delicious lime curd, using 5 small limes instead of the 3 lemons. Another variation is to use 1 lemon and 3 clementines – delicious at Christmas time when the clementines are in season. Don't substitute satsumas for clementines, by contrast they are utterly tasteless.

Strawberry & Elderflower Jam

This jam is heavenly eaten 'straight' on hot buttered toast, or with warm scones. It also forms the basis for many a wonderful pud.

Makes about 6 lb (2.7 kg)

---

3 lb (1.4 kg) strawberries, hulled
3 lb (1.4 kg) granulated sugar
juice of 1 lemon

1 handful of redcurrants, stripped from their stalks – these are optional, but help the set
3–4 handfuls of elderflowers

Leave the strawberries whole and put them into a large saucepan or jam pan. Add the sugar, lemon juice and redcurrants (if you are using them).

Carefully pull the tiny elderflowers off their stems; do this over the pan so that they fall straight in. Cover the pan and leave in a warm place for a couple of hours – I leave mine sitting on the Aga, or in one of the cooler ovens.

Then put the pan over a fairly gentle heat, and stir occasionally until the sugar has dissolved completely. Raise the heat, and boil fast. After 10–15 minutes' rapid boiling, spoon a small amount of syrup from the pan on to a small saucer and leave in the fridge for several minutes (take the pan off the heat while you are doing this so that the jam doesn't go on cooking); then push the jam on the saucer with the tip of your finger, if it wrinkles on the surface, you have a set. If it still looks runny, put the pan back on the heat and boil fast for a further 5 minutes, then draw off the heat again and repeat the test.

Cool the jam in the pan for about 20 minutes, then pot into warmed jars, cover with waxed paper discs, seal with cellophane and rubber bands and label. Store in a cool place. I get tremendous satisfaction from gazing at rows of pots of home-made jams and chutneys – a store cupboard complex!

Bramble Jelly

We get a wonderful crop of brambles, providing we don't get a spell of rainy weather just as they are about to ripen. Some years I can pick 7 or 8 lb (3.2–3.6 kg) afternoon after afternoon, and it is when they are in such abundance that I make bramble jelly. It is good on warm buttery scones, or in a Queen of Puddings (page 97).

Put as many brambles as you have into a large saucepan or jam pan and fill the pan with water to just come to the level of the fruit. Bring this to the boil and simmer gently, uncovered, for about 30 minutes. Draw the pan off the heat, cool, then strain through a jelly bag into a large bowl for several hours. I find it convenient to leave it overnight to drip.

Measure the juice back into the rinsed-out pan. For every 1 pint (600 ml) juice add 1 lb (450 g) granulated or preserving sugar. Put the pan with the juice and sugar in it over a gentle heat and stir until the sugar has completely dissolved. Then bring to a fast boil and boil furiously for 10 minutes. Draw the pan off the heat and spoon a little of the juice on to a saucer. Leave in the fridge for several minutes, then push the juice in the saucer with the tip of a finger. If it wrinkles, you have a set. If it doesn't, boil the juice fast again for another 5 minutes, then pull the pan off the heat and test again. Pot into warmed jars, cover with discs of waxed paper, seal with cellophane and rubber bands and label. Store in a cool place.

Blackcurrant & Blackcurrant Leaf Jam

Adding a handful of blackcurrant leaves to this jam imparts a fragrance and flavour which lifts it out of the realms of the ordinary into something special.

Makes about 9 lb (4 kg)

---

4 lb (1.8 kg) blackcurrants, stripped from their stalks
a large handful of blackcurrant leaves

4 lb (1.8 kg) granulated sugar

Put the blackcurrants, 2 pints (1.1 litres) water and the leaves together in a large saucepan or jam pan. Bring to a gentle simmer. Meanwhile warm the sugar. Simmer the blackcurrants until just squashable, then stir in the warm sugar – warming it helps it to dissolve quicker. Stir until the sugar has dissolved completely, then boil fast and furiously for 10 minutes; draw the pan off the heat and spoon a little of the jam on to a saucer. Leave in the fridge for several minutes. Then with your finger tip gently push the surface of the jam – if it wrinkles slightly, you have a set, if it doesn't and looks still runny, put the pan back on the heat for a further 5 minutes' fast boiling. Draw the pan off the heat and repeat the process. Fish out the leaves, and pot the jam into warmed jars; cover with discs of waxed paper, seal with cellophane and rubber bands and label.

Orange Marmalade

I love making marmalade, something I'm sure I've inherited from my mother! However, our tastes in marmalade differ. My mother likes to use all Seville oranges, giving a rather chunky, bitter type of preserve. I like a sweeter marmalade altogether, with finer peel; in fact I put the fruit through my food processor, getting almost a minced marmalade. I also like to experiment with flavours, and I never use just Seville oranges, which I find too bitter. I use grapefruit, lemons, and tangerines or clementines, as well.

Makes 11–12 lb (5–5.4 kg)

---

about 1½ lb (700 g) Seville oranges	1 grapefruit, 1 lemon, 4 clementines
about 1¼ lb (700 g) mixed other fruit, e.g.	6 lb (2.7 kg) granulated or preserving sugar

---

Put the fruit, whole, into a large saucepan or jam pan, add 4 pints (2.3 litres) water and bring to the boil. Simmer gently for several hours. I leave mine in the top left-hand oven of my 4-door Aga overnight. If I'm making it not on an Aga, I simmer for a few hours then leave it to sit overnight.

Remove the fruit from the pan, and cut each in half. Scoop all the pips out of the various fruit into a small saucepan. Pour about ½ pint (300 ml) water over the pips and simmer for 10–15 minutes. Strain this pip water into the water in the large pan.

Cut up the fruit to whatever size you like – this is the stage at which I put the fruit in my food processor, a little at a time, tipping the result into the large saucepan of water as it is ready, until all the fruit is minced. Add the sugar to the pan and put on a low heat. Stir until the sugar has dissolved completely, then boil very fast. After 10 minutes' fast boiling, pull the pan off the heat, and spoon a little of the marmalade on to a saucer. Leave in the fridge for several minutes. Then, with the tip of your finger, push the edge of the marmalade sample. If it wrinkles slightly, you have a set. If it is still runny, put the pan back on the heat, bring to the boil again, and boil furiously for a further 5 minutes. Draw the pan off the heat, and repeat the test. Then pot into warmed jars, cover with waxed paper discs, seal with cellophane and rubber bands and label.

No two batches of my marmalade ever taste quite the same, because I never use exactly the same fruits, but I rather like the variety. The total weight of the fruit should always be 3 lb (1.4 kg).

Mint Jelly

I love home-made mint jelly with roast lamb. It always reminds me of when Meriel, our third daughter, was born, as I spent the last few days before her birth making our windfall apples into mint jelly. I think I even left my long-suffering mother to pot the last batch, but so great was her relief at the arrival of Meriel (who kept us all hanging about for ages) that she didn't mind a bit!

This is ideal made with windfall apples. Cut the apples in quarters and put them into a large saucepan. Cover with water, and put on a moderate heat. Simmer gently for about 1 hour. Then strain through a jelly bag into a large bowl – I generally do this in the evening, leaving it to drip overnight.

Measure the apple juice into the rinsed-out large saucepan. To each 1 pint (600 ml) juice, add 1 lb (450 g) granulated sugar and 1 pint (600 ml) vinegar. I like to use white wine vinegar, but you can use any vinegar you like. Cider vinegar would be good for this recipe. Add to the pan 2–3 good handfuls of mint still on the stalks.

Put the pan on the heat and stir until the sugar has dissolved completely, then boil fast for 10 minutes. Draw the pan off the heat, and pour a little of the syrup on to a saucer. Leave in the fridge for several minutes, then gently push it with your finger tip. If it wrinkles slightly, your jelly will set. If it is at all runny, put the pan back on the heat and boil for a further 5 minutes, then pull it off the heat and test again. Fish out the mint.

Strip the leaves from another 2–3 handfuls of mint – my favourite is apple mint, but any mint will do. Chop the mint leaves finely, and stir them through the jelly. Pot into warmed jars, cover with waxed paper discs, seal with cellophane and rubber bands and label.

Apricot & Mint Jam

This is another good accompaniment for roast lamb or grilled lamb chops.

Makes about 6 lb (2.7 kg)

1½ lb (700 g) good dried apricots	2 handfuls of mint on the stems
1 pint (600 ml) white wine vinegar	2 handfuls of mint, with the leaves stripped from the stems, and finely chopped
3 lb (1.4 kg) granulated sugar	

Chop the apricots quite small, and put them into a large saucepan together with 2 pints (1.1 litres) water and the vinegar. Soak for a couple of hours then, over a gentle heat, bring to simmering point. Cover the pan and simmer for 1½ hours.

Warm the sugar while the apricots are simmering, and when they are very soft, add the sugar and the mint on the stalks to the pan. Stir until the sugar has dissolved completely, then boil fast for 10 minutes. Draw the pan off the heat and spoon a little of the liquid on to a saucer. Leave in the fridge for several minutes, then push with the tip of your finger; if it wrinkles, the jam will set. If it is still runny, boil fast for a further 5 minutes, and test again. Fish out the mint stems.

Stir the finely chopped mint into the jam, and pot into warmed jars. Cover with discs of waxed paper, seal with cellophane and rubber bands and label.

Spicy Plum Jam

We make this to serve with roast venison, but it would be just as good as an accompaniment to roast lamb, or grilled lamb chops. It is a recipe to make when plums are plentiful and cheap or, better still, if you grow your own. But I think it needs rather sharp-flavoured plums; Victorias would be too sweet.

Makes about 7 lb (3.2 kg)

4 lb (1.8 kg) plums, cut in half but with their stones left in	*1 stick of cinnamon*
	1 rounded dessertspoon ground mixed spice
1 pint (600ml) white wine vinegar	*4 lb (1.8 kg) granulated sugar*

Put the halved plums, stones and all, into a large saucepan or jam pan together with the vinegar, cinnamon stick and mixed spice. Bring to a gentle simmer, and cook for 30 minutes, with a lid on the saucepan. Warm the sugar during this time.

Draw the pan off the heat and, using a metal slotted spoon, scoop out all the stones you can. They obligingly float to the surface, most of them, so this job isn't as arduous as it sounds!

Add the sugar to the pan, put on a gentle heat, uncovered, and stir until the sugar has completely dissolved. Then boil fast for 10 minutes. Draw the pan off the heat, spoon a little of the juice on to a saucer, and leave in the fridge for several minutes. Then push with your finger tip – if the juice wrinkles, you have a set. If it is still runny, boil the contents of the saucepan again for 5 minutes. Draw off the heat and repeat the test. Pot into warmed pots, cover with waxed paper discs, seal with cellophane and rubber bands and label.

Cumberland Jelly

Oh this is so good! It is also very versatile, as it enhances any ham dish, hot or cold, or venison, roast duck, cold turkey or chicken. It also makes a lovely present. It keeps for 3–4 weeks in the fridge.

Makes about 2 lb (900 g)

---

8 oz (225 g) redcurrant jelly	*grated rind and juice of*
1 level tablespoon dry	*1 orange*
mustard powder	*grated rind and juice of*
½ pint (300 ml) port	*1 lemon*
½ oz (15 g) gelatine	

Put the redcurrant jelly and mustard powder into a saucepan and gradually stir in the port. As you stir, the mustard will become smooth; then sprinkle over the gelatine. Add the grated orange and lemon rinds, and the orange and lemon juices, and put the pan on a gentle heat. Heat, stirring occasionally, until the redcurrant jelly has melted, and the granules of gelatine dissolved. Pour into warmed jars, or bowl, and leave until it cools, and sets. Cover with cling film and store in the fridge.

Home-made Mustard

Home-made mustard is a useful item to have on your shelves. We put honey in ours, but you could put in muscovado sugar if you prefer. I think it is worth while making quite a lot at one time – after all, it keeps perfectly. So we make up 3 lb (1.4 kg) mustard seeds at a time.

Makes about 4 lb (1.8 kg)

1½ lb (700 g) white mustard seeds (they are actually pale yellow) 1½ lb (700 g) red mustard seeds	2 tablespoons honey vinegar to cover the seeds – we use red wine vinegar, but you can use any type of vinegar

Put the mustard seeds into a large bowl (not a metal one) and add the honey (it won't be possible to blend it in properly at this stage). Fill the bowl with vinegar to just cover the seeds. Leave for 3 days, covered with cling film. From time to time, stir the mustard and the honey will gradually melt into the mustard mixture. Store in screw-topped jars.

Apple & Raisin Chutney

This is a recipe to make when there is a glut of apples available, or when apples are very cheap. I use windfall eaters. Any kind of vinegar will do.

Makes about 6 lb (2.7 kg)

3 lb (1.4 kg) apples, weighed after peeling and coring

1½ lb (700 g) onions, peeled and thinly sliced

1 lb (450 g) sultanas

2 rounded teaspoons ground ginger

1 rounded teaspoon ground mixed spice

1 level teaspoon salt

2 lb (900 g) dark soft brown sugar, or muscovado sugar

2 pints (1.1 litres) vinegar

Chop the peeled and cored apples and put into a large saucepan or jam pan together with all the other ingredients. Bring to the boil and simmer, with the pan uncovered, for 1½ hours. Pot into warmed jars, cover with waxed paper discs and cellophane, as for jam.

Green Tomato Chutney

We always seem to have an abundance of green tomatoes, as I'm sure anyone does who grows them, and they sell here in Skye for next to nothing. I think green tomato chutney is my favourite of all chutneys. This is Katherine Robertson's recipe, with one or two small adaptations of mine. Katherine is part of our small team here at Kinloch, really one of the family.

Makes about 5 lb (2.3 kg)

3 lb (1.4 kg) green tomatoes
6 onions
3 large cooking apples
1 pint (600 ml) vinegar
8 oz (225 g) raisins
1 lb (450 g) soft dark
   brown sugar – I like to
   use muscovado sugar

1 rounded teaspoon ground
   ginger
1 rounded tablespoon salt
1 level teaspoon freshly
   ground black pepper
1 oz (25 g) pickling spice

Slice the tomatoes. Skin and slice the onions. Put them all in a large bowl, and sprinkle the salt over them. Leave overnight.

Next day, drain away the juice which will have seeped out of the tomatoes. Peel, core and chop the apples and put them and all the other ingredients into a large saucepan or jam pan. Bring to the boil and simmer gently for about 2 hours, until the chutney is thick and a rich brown colour. Pot into warmed jars, cover each with a disc of waxed paper, seal with cellophane and rubber bands and label. Don't eat this chutney for 3–4 weeks, as the flavour mellows.

Mincemeat

It is only in the last few years that I have been making mincemeat. I always intended making it each year, but somehow thought it was a great labour and never quite did get around to it. If only I had! There is a world of difference between home-made mincemeat and the commercial sort. And my image of the making of it being an all day affair was quite wrong – once the ingredients are collected together it doesn't take a minute to put together. There are endless variations on mincemeat – like chutneys and marmalades – and I always love being given a pot of someone else's. There are several puddings in which mincemeat features – such as the delicious Apple and Mincemeat Meringue Pie (page 52) and Baked Apples Stuffed with Mincemeat, with Orange Sabayon Sauce (page 62). But, most of all, mincemeat is used for making mince pies. No one in the world makes better mince pies than Peter Macpherson.

Makes about 6 lb (2.7 kg)

12 oz (350 g) raisins
8 oz (225 g) sultanas
8 oz (225g) currants
4 oz (125 g) chopped mixed peel
4 oz (125 g) chopped blanched almonds
8 oz (225 g) shredded suet
1 lb (450 g) soft dark brown sugar, I like to use muscovado
12 oz (350 g) apples (Cox's are best) with their skins on, cored and chopped

grated rind of 2 lemons
juice of 1 lemon
grated rind of 2 oranges
juice of 1 orange
4 fl oz (125 ml) brandy
1 level teaspoon ground cinnamon
1 rounded teaspoon grated nutmeg
1 rounded teaspoon ground allspice

Mix all the ingredients together in a large bowl (not a metal bowl). Cover with cling film and leave for a week, giving the occasional stir. After a week, pot into jars and cover. Keep for a further 2 weeks before using.

Vanilla Fudge

After dinner, in the hotel, we put a plate of fudge beside the coffee in the drawing room. It is apparently loved by the guests. This, I feel, is true appreciation because they have all had a fairly full dinner before they get to the coffee and fudge stage!

Makes about 2 lb (900 g)

1 lb (450 g) granulated sugar	*¼ pint (150 ml) condensed milk*
4 oz (125 g) butter	*a few drops of vanilla essence*
¼ pint (150 ml) milk	

Butter a tin about 6 × 8 in (15 × 20 cm) and line it with siliconised paper. Put all the ingredients together in a saucepan. Stir over a low heat until the sugar has dissolved completely. Then bring to the boil, and boil until it reaches 250°F (120°C) on a sugar thermometer. Stir the fudge all the time as it boils. If you haven't got a sugar thermometer, have a mug or bowl of cold water to hand and when the mixture is beginning to come away from the sides of the pan as it boils, draw the pan off the heat and drop a little of the mixture into the cold water. As it hits the water, it should form a soft ball. When it reaches the correct temperature, remove from the heat, and stir vigorously for 3–5 minutes; it will thicken as it cools. Pour the fudge into the lined tin and leave to set. As it cools, cut it into squares with a sharp knife.

By the way, if you are making lots of fudge, perhaps for a batch of presents or for a sale of work, it freezes very well.

Chocolate Fudge

I just don't know which I prefer – chocolate or vanilla fudge. A mixture of pieces of both flavours makes a lovely present for those with a sweet tooth, like my father.

Makes about 30 1-inch (2.5 cm) squares

1 14-oz (400-g) tin condensed milk	*12 oz (350 g) granulated sugar*
5 oz (150 g) butter	*1 rounded tablespoon cocoa*
	a few drops vanilla essence

Butter a tin about 6 × 8 in (15 × 20 cm) and line it with a piece of siliconised paper.

Put all the ingredients together in a saucepan and stir over a gentle heat until the sugar has dissolved completely. Then boil and stir continuously until the mixture thickens as it boils. Pull the pan off the heat and beat really hard for 1 minute, then pour into the prepared tin. When it hardens and sets, cut into squares in the tin.

Chocolate & Coconut Squares

These are extremely easy to put together, and very good to eat. I like the contrast between the coconut and the rich chocolatey mixture underneath. The brandy is optional!

Makes 20–24

---

4 oz (125 g) dark chocolate
4 oz (125 g) butter
6 oz (175 g) digestive biscuits, crushed to fine crumbs – if you have a food processor it is ideal for this

3 tablespoons brandy, optional
2 oz (50 g) desiccated coconut

Lightly butter a tin about 6 × 8 in (15 × 20 cm) and press a piece of siliconised paper into it. Melt together over a very low heat the butter and chocolate. Stir the digestive crumbs into this mixture, and the brandy. Pour it evenly into the paper-lined tray, and sprinkle the coconut over the surface. As the chocolate and butter mixture sets, the coconut sets into it. As it hardens, cut it into small squares, about 1 in (2.5 cm) in size. Don't keep these in the fridge, because the chocolate takes on a sort of 'bloom'; store them in an airtight container in a cool place.

Peppermint & Chocolate Creams

These are so easy to make, that even young children can produce them. But no matter how easy they are, they are delicious, peppermint and chocolate going so very well together. They are ideal for presents.

1 egg white
1 lb (450 g) icing sugar
1–2 teaspoons peppermint
  essence, the amount does
rather depend on how
strong you like peppermint
4 oz (125 g) good dark
chocolate

Whisk the egg white in a bowl until it is frothy. Sieve the icing sugar in, add the peppermint essence and mix all together until you have a stiff paste.

Sieve a little extra icing sugar on to a working surface, and dust a rolling pin also with sieved icing sugar. Roll the peppermint paste out, to a thickness of $\frac{1}{4}$ in (0.5 cm). Cut it with a small cutter, mine is just over 1 in (2.5 cm) in diameter. Put the peppermint creams on a tray with a piece of siliconised paper on it and leave to dry out for an hour or so.

Meanwhile, break up the chocolate into a small bowl, and put the bowl over a saucepan of very hot water – but not boiling. As the squares of chocolate soften, beat with a small palette knife then leave to cool. Using the small palette knife, smear melted chocolate on each peppermint cream, leaving a little swirl towards the centre of each. It is impossible to get them all identical, but try to be as neat as you can. Avoid storing them in the fridge, because the chocolate will develop a sort of bloom, a dusty look. Keep them in an airtight tin until you are ready to package them.

Treacle Toffee

Treacle toffee always reminds me of Hallowe'en and Bonfire Night. When we were young, and happened to be at my Aunt Christine's house for Guy Fawkes' night, we used to have treacle toffee. As it is a great favourite with our girls it is something I make as a contribution to the sweet tin.

Have a saucepan of boiling water, and dip the tablespoon into it before dipping it into the treacle tin. The treacle will slip off easily. The same applies to measuring golden syrup.

Makes 24–30 pieces

1 lb (450 g) demerara sugar	*1 14-oz (400-g) tin*
3 tablespoons black treacle	*condensed milk*
3 tablespoons golden syrup	*4 oz (125 g) butter*
	½ teaspoon vanilla essence

Put all the ingredients into a saucepan except the vanilla essence. Stir over a gentle heat until the sugar has dissolved. Bring to the boil, and boil for 15–20 minutes, then pull the pan off the heat, and drop a little of the toffee into a small bowl of cold water; it should crack, i.e. be brittle in the water. When it reaches this stage, stir in the vanilla essence and pour into a buttered tin, lined with a piece of siliconised paper. Leave to set and when it is nearly cold mark into squares with a sharp knife. Cut and break into squares, and wrap each in greaseproof paper.

Cointreau & Chocolate Marzipan Balls

I always make marzipan for my Christmas cakes. A lot of people think this is a waste of time, and that bought marzipan is just as good, but I really don't agree. It doesn't take long to make and it keeps, wrapped in cling film in the fridge, until you are ready to use it. These sweets are ambrosial.

Makes about 20

---

4 oz (125 g) icing sugar	*1 teaspoon lemon juice*
4 oz (125 g) caster sugar	*1 dessertspoon Cointreau*
8 oz (225 g) ground almonds	*finely grated rind of 1 large orange*
1 egg, beaten	*4 oz (125 g) dark chocolate*

Sieve the icing sugar into a bowl. Add the caster sugar, and sieve the ground almonds into the bowl. Using a wooden spoon, work into the dry ingredients the beaten egg and lemon juice, the Cointreau and the grated orange rind. Wrap the paste, in a ball, in cling film and leave in the fridge for several hours.

Break up the chocolate into a small bowl and put the bowl over a saucepan of very hot water – but not boiling. Stir the chocolate occasionally as it melts, then let it cool. Then with a little sieved icing sugar on the palms of your hands, to prevent the mixture from sticking too much as you work, take 1 teaspoon of the paste at a time and roll into balls. Dip half of each ball into the melted chocolate, and put them on to a tray with a piece of siliconised paper on it. Leave until the chocolate is set. Then arrange them in boxes or on trays. Don't keep them in the fridge, because the chocolate takes on a 'bloom'; keep them in a cool place in an airtight container until you are ready to use them.

Chocolate Truffles – Very Rich

I make these for presents for special people. They are for me the ultimate in chocolate sweets. The Angostura bitters in the recipe comes from Godfrey, my husband, who apparently was a connoisseur of truffle-making in his youth! I always use Bournville chocolate – please don't use chocolate flavouring or cake covering, it would be a total waste.

Makes 16–18

8 oz (225 g) dark chocolate 1 level teaspoon instant coffee stirred into 1 tablespoon boiling water	4 oz (125 g) butter, preferably unsalted a few drops of Angostura bitters cocoa powder

Break up the chocolate into a bowl, and put the coffee in with it. Put the bowl over a saucepan of gently simmering water, until the chocolate is melted. Take the bowl off the pan, and beat in the butter, bit by bit. Then beat in the Angostura bitters. Put the bowl in a cool place for several hours, until the chocolate and butter mixture is quite hard.

On a working surface, put about 2 tablespoons cocoa, and rub some into the palms of your hands. Using a teaspoon, scoop up some of the hard mixture and roll it into even-sized balls between the palms of your hands. Then roll each ball in cocoa, and put into a container. Keep them in the fridge until you are ready to package them. As you roll them, the palms of your hands will become warmer and so melt the mixture a bit, and this job can be quite a messy one, but it is well worth it!

Wendy's Fudge Chocolate Squares

These are good, either cut into larger squares and eaten at tea-time, or cut into smaller squares and served as an after-dinner sweet.

---

6 oz (175 g) caster sugar	7½-oz (213-g) packet
4 oz (125 g) butter	digestive biscuits
2 tablespoons golden syrup	6 oz (175 g) chocolate,
7-oz (200-g) tin condensed	either milk chocolate or
milk	plain

Put the sugar, butter, syrup and condensed milk into a saucepan over a low heat and melt. When the butter has melted and the sugar dissolved, boil for 5–8 minutes.

Crush the biscuits into crumbs, and after the boiling time is up remove the saucepan from the heat and stir in the crumbs thoroughly. Grease a baking tin (or line it with a piece of siliconised paper) measuring about 8 × 10 in (20 × 30 cm). Pour the mixture into it and leave to cool.

Meanwhile, break the chocolate into a small bowl, and put the bowl over a saucepan of very gently simmering water until the chocolate is soft. Spread it evenly over the cooled fudgey biscuit mixture in the tin, and when that too has cooled divide into squares. You will get about 14–16 large squares, or about 24 smaller ones from this amount.

Pudding Cakes, Cakes & Biscuits

There are many delicious recipes for cakes which really need to be eaten with a fork, and which make perfect puddings. Most people have a weakness for cake and to serve it as a pudding is to indulge them without adding an extra meal. Thanks to siliconised paper, there need never be a danger of cakes sticking to the tins after cooking. I know that there are non-stick cake tins available, but I've never found that they stay non-stick for very long. So I always line them.

Extremely Rich Chocolate & Almond Cake

This cake is too rich for eating other than as a pudding at the end of a dinner party. It evolved during the course of a recent summer and rapidly became a firm favourite on the menu at Kinloch. The cake is so rich and moist that it needs only a dusting of icing sugar on top, and a bowl of unsweetened whipped cream handed round with it. There is grated orange rind in the cake, and the sharp, fresh orange flavour is what makes it distinctive.

Serves 8

---

6 oz (175 g) good, dark chocolate	6 oz (175 g) ground almonds, sieved
6 oz (175 g) butter	grated rind of 1 large orange
6 oz (175 g) caster sugar	1 rounded tablespoon icing sugar
3 large eggs	

Line an 8 in (20 cm) cake tin with siliconised paper, or, if you are using a non-stick tin, just put a disc of paper in the bottom.

Break the chocolate into a small bowl, and put the bowl over a small saucepan of gently simmering water, until the chocolate melts. Leave it to cool.

Put the butter in another bowl and, using a hand-held electric whisk, beat until the butter is creamy, then gradually add the caster sugar, beating until it is all incorporated and the mixture is pale and fluffy. Beat in the eggs one by one, beating really well each time, then stir in the cooled, melted chocolate and the sieved ground almonds and grated orange rind.

Pour and scrape the mixture into the prepared cake tin and bake in a low to moderate oven, 325°F (170°C) Gas mark 3 (bottom of the bottom right-hand oven, in a 4-door

134

Aga) for about 50 minutes. Remove from the oven and leave in the tin for 10 minutes or so, then turn on to a wire cooling rack until cold. Before serving, sieve the icing sugar over the surface, and hand round a bowl of whipped cream with it.

This cake can be made 2–3 days ahead; in fact, it improves with keeping.

Walnut Sponge with Lemon Curd Cream

This pudding is very easy to make, and the combined flavours and textures of the lightest of sponges, walnuts, lemon and cream are exquisite. It is even better when we make it using Lemon and Elderflower Curd (page 110).

Serves 8

4 oz (125 g) walnuts	Sauce:
3 large eggs	*½ pint (300 ml) double*
3 oz (75 g) caster sugar	*cream, whipped*
3 oz (75 g) self-raising flour	*8 oz (225 g) home-made*
icing sugar	*lemon curd*

Line an 8 in (20 cm) cake tin with siliconised paper, or, if you are using a non-stick tin, just put a disc of paper in the bottom. Put the walnuts in a polythene bag and break them up with a rolling pin.

Put the eggs into a large bowl, and whisk (I use a hand-held electric whisk) until they are beginning to thicken. Then gradually add the caster sugar and continue whisking until the mixture is very thick and pale – thick enough to write a squiggle with the end of the whisk. This takes about 7–10 minutes.

Sieve the self-raising flour into a bowl and then sieve it

again, little by little, on to the cake mixture, folding it in as quickly and as thoroughly as you can. I find a large metal slotted spoon ideal for this job, be it folding flour into a cake, or egg whites into a mousse. Lastly, fold in the broken walnuts. Pour the cake mixture into the prepared tin and bake in a moderate oven, 350°F (180°C) Gas mark 4 (middle of the bottom right-hand oven of a 4-door Aga) for 25–30 minutes. If cooked, it should be just beginning to come away from the sides of the tin. Remove the tin from the oven, leave for 2–3 minutes, then turn the cake on to a cooling rack.

When the cake is quite cold, put it on a serving plate and dust the top with a little sieved icing sugar. For the sauce, fold together the whipped cream and the lemon curd, and put it into a glass or china bowl to serve with the cake.

This cake really should be made the day it is to be eaten. But it does freeze well, so to save time you can make it ahead and freeze it.

Coffee & Praline Gâteau

This is a delicious mixture of fudgey coffee icing, cream filling, light sponge cake, and slightly crunchy praline. As with the walnut sponge, it really should be made the day it is to be eaten, but it could, at a pinch, be made the day before, because any left-overs seem to taste very good the next day!

Serves 8

Praline:
2 oz (50 g) granulated sugar
1 oz (25 g) almonds, whole or flaked
Cake:
3 large eggs
3 oz (75 g) caster sugar
3 oz (75 g) self-raising flour
1 level tablespoon instant coffee powder
Butter cream:
4 oz (125 g) butter

3 oz (75 g) icing sugar, sieved
1 level dessertspoon instant coffee powder
Icing:
1 oz (25 g) granulated sugar
2 oz (50 g) butter
8 oz (225 g) icing sugar, sieved
1 level dessertspoon instant coffee powder

To make the praline put the sugar and almonds together in a saucepan over a moderate to high heat, and shake the saucepan as the sugar begins to dissolve. When the sugar has dissolved completely and there is a golden syrup in the pan, pour on to a well-greased baking sheet and leave to cool and harden. When it is quite cold, cover the praline with a piece of greaseproof paper and bash it with a rolling pin into large crumb-sized bits. This praline keeps well in a screw-topped jar.

Line an 8 in (20 cm) cake tin with siliconised paper. Put the eggs in a large bowl and whisk them until they are just beginning to thicken. Gradually add the caster sugar, whisking all together until the mixture is so thick that you can trace a squiggle off the end of the whisk, and it remains on top of the mixture. This takes about 7–10 minutes with a hand-held electric whisk.

Sieve the flour and coffee powder on to a plate or into a bowl, and sieve it again on to the cake mixture – folding it in with a large metal spoon as quickly and thoroughly as possible. Pour the cake mixture into the prepared tin and bake in a moderate oven, 350°F (180°C) Gas mark 4 (middle of the bottom right-hand oven in a 4-door Aga) for 25–30 minutes, until the cake is beginning to come away from the sides of the tin. Cool in the tin for 2–3 minutes, then turn on to a cooling rack until quite cold. Using a serrated knife, cut the cake in half, and put the bottom half on a serving plate.

For the butter cream, beat the butter, gradually adding the sieved icing sugar and the coffee powder, and beating all together until light and fluffy. Spread this evenly over the bottom half of the cake, and put the other half on top.

Finally, make the fudge icing. Put $\frac{1}{4}$ pint (150 ml) water, the granulated sugar and the butter together in a small saucepan. Place over a gentle heat until the sugar has dissolved and the butter melted, then turn up the heat and boil fast for about 5 minutes. Sieve the icing sugar into a bowl with the coffee powder. Stir in the boiled sugar and butter syrup, and beat from time to time as it cools. If it gets too stiff as it cools, add a very little boiling water. Spread this fudgey icing over the top and sides of the cake, and sprinkle the praline over the surface.

We sometimes make twice the amount of butter cream and, using a large star nozzle, pipe large rosettes round the top of the cake. If you want to make it a real showpiece, pipe rosettes round the bottom of the cake too – by now the cake will serve 10 people, and will have really earned its title of gâteau!

Cinnamon &
Raspberry Cream Sponge Cake

Cinnamon enhances the flavour of raspberries and this pudding cake is one of my favourites when raspberries are in season. The cake should be made the same day it is to be eaten, but if you are going to be very rushed, make the cake ahead and freeze it, then put it together with the raspberries and cream on the day. It is easy and quick to make, with the cake mixture all in one bowl, so it doesn't involve endless washing up afterwards.

Serves 8

3 large eggs
5 oz (150 g) caster sugar
3 oz (75 g) self-raising flour
1 rounded dessertspoon
ground cinnamon
¾ pint (425 ml) double
cream

about 12 oz (350 g)
raspberries, keeping about
20 on one side for
decorating if you like
1 dessertspoon icing sugar

Line the bottom and sides of an 8 in (20 cm) cake tin with siliconised paper, or, if you are using a non-stick tin, just put a disc of paper in the bottom.

Put the eggs into a large bowl and whisk until they are just beginning to thicken, then gradually add 3 oz (75 g) caster sugar. Whisk all together until the mixture is so thick that you can trace a squiggle with the end of the whisk on top of the mixture and it will stay there – this takes about 7–10 minutes. Sieve together into a bowl or on to a large plate the self-raising flour and cinnamon. Then sieve it again on to the egg mixture and fold it into the mixture using a large metal spoon, folding as quickly and thoroughly as possible. Pour the cake mixture into the prepared tin and bake in a moderate oven, 350°F (180°C)

Gas mark 4 (the middle of the bottom right-hand oven of a 4-door Aga) for 25–30 minutes, or until the sides of the cake are just beginning to come away from the sides of the tin. Remove from the oven and leave in its tin for 2–3 minutes. Then turn on to a cooling rack until completely cold. When it is quite cold, cut in half, using a serrated knife.

Whip the cream and remaining caster sugar together until fairly stiff, then put half the sweetened whipped cream into another bowl and whip it a bit stiffer – this is going to be piped, so it needs to be rather stiffer. Keep about 20 raspberries on one side for decorating and fold the rest into the not-so-stiffly-whipped cream. Cover the bottom half of the cinnamon sponge with this. Level the surface of the raspberry and cream filling as much as possible, then put the other half of the cake on top. Sieve the icing sugar over the surface. Fill a large piping bag with a star nozzle with the remaining cream and pipe large rosettes (touching each other) round the edge of the top of the cake. Tuck the reserved raspberries round the inside and outside of the rosettes.

Lemon Griestorte

This lovely lemony cake has a delicious slightly grainy texture. It can be filled either with a mixture of lemon curd and whipped cream, or with strawberries or raspberries and whipped cream. The recipe was given to me by my sister Olivia, who in turn got it from Annie Langford.

Serves 6–8

---

3 eggs, separated
4 oz (125 g) caster sugar
grated rind of 1 lemon
juice of ½ lemon
½ oz (15 g) ground almonds
2 oz (50 g) fine semolina
icing sugar

Filling.
½ pint (300 ml) double
  cream, whipped fairly
  stiffly
8 oz (225 g) lemon curd
  (home-made) or ¾–1 lb
  (350–450 g) fruit, such
  as raspberries or
  strawberries

Grease an 8 in (20 cm) cake tin and line it with siliconised paper. Beat the egg yolks, gradually adding the caster sugar, and beat until thick and mousse-like. Add the lemon rind and juice, and beat again. Sieve the ground almonds and fold them and the semolina into the yolk mixture. Whisk the egg whites until very stiff and fold them in, using a large metal spoon, as quickly and thoroughly as possible. Put the mixture into the prepared cake tin and bake in a low to moderate oven, 325°F (170°C) Gas mark 3 (bottom of the bottom right-hand oven of a 4-door Aga) for 30–40 minutes. Remove from the oven, leave in the tin for a couple of minutes, then turn on to a wire rack to cool.

When it is cold, split the cake with a serrated knife, put the bottom half on a serving plate, and fill with the cream and either lemon curd or fruit. Put the other half on top, and dust with sieved icing sugar before serving.

Banana, Strawberry Jam & Cream Swiss Roll

This is a pudding cake, by which I mean that you need a spoon and fork to eat it. It is a sort of schoolboy's dream come true, with the lightest of sponge Swiss rolls, oozing with cream, strawberry jam and bananas.

Serves 6–8 generously

---

3 large eggs
3 oz (75 g) caster sugar
a few drops of vanilla
  essence
3 oz (75 g) self-raising flour
extra caster sugar

8 oz (225 g) strawberry
  jam, preferably home-
  made
½ pint (300 ml) double
  cream, whipped fairly
  stiffly
3 bananas

Lightly grease a Swiss roll tin about 8 by 12 in (20 by 30 cm), and cover it with a piece of siliconised paper.

Put the eggs in a bowl and whisk them until they are just beginning to thicken. Then add the caster sugar and vanilla essence gradually, whisking together until the mixture is so thick that you can trail a squiggle from the end of the whisk and it holds its shape on top of the mixture. This takes about 7–10 minutes.

Sieve the flour into a bowl, then sieve it again on to the egg mixture. Using a large metal spoon, fold it in as quickly and thoroughly as possible. Pour this mixture into the prepared Swiss roll tin, smooth evenly, and bake in a moderate oven, 350°F (180°C) Gas mark 4 (middle of the bottom right-hand oven of a 4-door Aga) for 15 minutes. Spread another piece of siliconised paper on to a table or work surface, and sprinkle it with caster sugar. When the cooking time is up, remove the tin from the oven and tip the cake on to the sugared paper. Carefully peel off the paper it has cooked in and roll the cake up; put the roll on a wire rack to cool.

When the Swiss roll is quite cold, unroll it and spread the strawberry jam over the inside. Spread the whipped cream on top of the jam, then peel and slice the bananas (this has to be done at the last minute to stop the banana slices going brown) and spread the slices as evenly as possible over the cream. Roll the Swiss roll up again and put it on a serving dish. Sprinkle with a little caster sugar.

Parsnip Cake

This is a variation on my carrot cake recipe, using parsnips instead of carrots. Anyone eating it and not knowing the ingredients would be even more mystified than with carrot cake! It is delicious but I'm still not brave enough to put 'Carrot or Parsnip Cake' on the menu – we still call it Kinloch Gâteau.

Serves 8

just under ½ pint (300 ml) *sunflower seed oil*	*1 level teaspoon ground cinnamon*
12 oz (350 g) caster sugar	*½ level teaspoon salt*
3 eggs	*8 oz (225 g) grated raw*
6 oz (175 g) plain flour	*parsnips*
1 level teaspoon bicarbonate of soda	Filling and icing:
1 level teaspoon baking powder	*6 oz (175 g) cream cheese*
	6 oz (175 g) butter
	8 oz (225 g) icing sugar
	1 teaspoon vanilla essence

Line the sides and bottom of an 8 in (20 cm) cake tin with siliconised paper.

Put the sunflower seed oil into a large bowl and add the caster sugar, whisking all together thoroughly. Add the eggs, one by one, whisking well between each one. Then stir in the sieved flour, bicarbonate of soda, baking powder, cinnamon and salt and lastly the grated parsnips. Put the mixture into the prepared cake tin, and bake in a moderate oven, 350°F (180°C) Gas mark 4 (middle of the bottom right-hand oven of a 4-door Aga) for about 45–50 minutes. Test to see if the cake is cooked by pushing a skewer into the middle; if it comes out clean the cake is cooked, if the skewer has sticky mixture on it, put the cake back for a further few minutes. Turn the cake on to a wire rack to cool. When the cake is quite cold, cut in half, using a serrated knife.

If you have a food processor put the cream cheese and butter into it and whizz until smooth. Then add the icing sugar and vanilla essence and whizz until there are no lumps of icing sugar, and you have a smooth butter cream.

If you don't have a food processor, beat the butter and cream cheese together in a bowl, and sieve the icing sugar spoonful by spoonful into it, beating well until it is all incorporated. Beat in the vanilla essence.

Spread the bottom half of the cake with butter cream, put the other half on top, and cover the top and sides of the cake with the rest of the butter cream.

The cake is actually better if made 3–4 days in advance, and kept in an airtight container. It freezes well unfilled, but I wouldn't freeze the filled and iced cake for more than 3 weeks, because I find that after 3–4 weeks vanilla essence takes on an unpleasantly oily taste.

Hazelnut & Chocolate Cream Gâteau

Somehow hazelnuts and chocolate were meant to go together.

Serves 8

---

3 large eggs	8 oz (225 g) plain chocolate
3 oz (75 g) caster sugar	¾ pint (425 ml) double
2 oz (50 g) self-raising flour	cream
2 oz (50 g) ground	icing sugar
hazelnuts	

Line two sandwich tins, about 7–8 in (18–20 cm) in diameter, with siliconised paper.

Put the eggs into a large bowl and whisk them until they are just beginning to thicken. Then gradually add the sugar, whisking until the mixture is very thick, thick enough so that you can trail a squiggle off the end of the whisk on to the mixture and it stays on top. This takes about 7–10 minutes.

Sieve the flour and hazelnuts into a bowl, then sieve them again on to the mixture, folding them in with a large metal spoon, as quickly and thoroughly as possible. Pour this mixture into the prepared cake tins, and bake in a moderate oven 350°F (180°C) Gas mark 4 (middle of the bottom right-hand oven in a 4-door Aga) for between 15 and 20 minutes, until the sides of the cakes are just beginning to come away from the tins. Remove from the oven, leave in the tins for a couple of minutes, then turn on to wire racks to cool.

With a potato peeler, shave about 2 tablespoons from the chocolate on to a small plate or saucer. Keep in the larder or a cool place.

Break the rest of the chocolate into a small bowl, and put the bowl over a small saucepan of gently simmering water for just long enough to melt the chocolate. Then remove the bowl from the heat and stir the chocolate until it is a smooth cream. Leave until completely cold. Whip the cream until fairly stiff. Remove about a third of the amount into a smaller bowl, and whip a bit stiffer; this smaller amount is for piping on top of the finished cake.

Gently fold together the cooled melted chocolate and the larger portion of whipped cream, and spread this over the bottom half of the hazelnut sponge, on a serving plate. Cover with the other half, and sieve a little icing sugar over the surface.

Fill a piping bag, fitted with a fluted nozzle, with the stiffer whipped cream, and pipe rosettes round the edge of the top of the cake. Cover the whole surface, rosettes and all, with the shavings of chocolate. To serve this cake, cut it with a serrated knife.

Chestnut & Chocolate Cream Sponge

There is a great contrast in this pudding cake between the featherlight chocolate sponge, and the rich, gooey filling. Probably because chestnuts mean winter to me, I always think of this as being a Christmas-time party pud.

Serves 8

---

3 large eggs
3 oz (75 g) caster sugar
2½ oz (65 g) self-raising
* flour*
1 rounded tablespoon cocoa
Filling:
8 oz (225 g) plain chocolate

15 oz (425 g) tin sweetened
* chestnut purée*
For the top of the cake:
about ⅓ pint (200 ml)
* double cream, whipped*
* fairly stiffly*
about 6 marrons glacés,
* optional*

Lightly grease 2 sandwich tins, about 8 in (20 cm) in diameter, and line them with siliconised paper.

Put the eggs in a large bowl and whisk them until they are just thickening, then whisk in the sugar, gradually. Continue whisking for about 7–10 minutes, until the mixture is so thick that you can trail a squiggle from the end of the whisk on the surface of the mixture and it holds its shape.

Sieve together the flour and cocoa into a bowl, and sieve it again on to the egg mixture. As you sieve, bit by bit fold it in using a large metal spoon, as quickly and thoroughly as possible. Divide this mixture between the sandwich tins and bake in a moderate oven, 350°F (180°C) Gas mark 4 (middle of the bottom right-hand oven of a 4-door Aga) for about 15–20 minutes. The cake is cooked when the sides are just beginning to shrink away from the tins. Remove from the oven and leave in the tins for a couple of minutes, then turn on to a wire rack to cool, peeling off the paper.

Using a potato peeler, shave about 1 rounded table-spoon chocolate from the block. Shave it on to a saucer, and keep in a cool place. Break the rest of the chocolate into a small bowl and put the bowl over a saucepan of gently simmering water for just long enough to melt the chocolate. Then remove from the heat, stir to a creamy consistency and set aside.

If you have a food processor, tip the sweetened chestnut purée into it and whizz, adding the chocolate, until you have a smooth cream. If you don't have a food processor, put the chestnut purée into a bowl and break it down with a wooden spoon; add the melted chocolate to it and mix and beat together until it is as smooth as you can get it.

Put one of the cooled cakes on to a serving plate and cover with this chocolate and chestnut purée. Put the other cake on top – the filling is nice and deep. Spread whipped cream over the top of the cake, and sprinkle the chocolate shavings over the cream. If you are using marrons glacés, cut them in half and arrange them around the edge of the cake.

Vanilla Biscuits

I find these disappear so fast that if I put a plateful on the tea table there never seem to be any left to put away for the next day. They don't take long to make, either.

Makes 18–20 biscuits

---

4 oz (125 g) butter
3 oz (75 g) caster sugar
a few drops of vanilla
essence

5 oz (150 g) plain flour
a little more caster sugar to
sprinkle on top

Put the butter into a bowl (or a food processor) and beat, adding the sugar gradually. Beat until creamy, then add the vanilla essence. Sieve the flour and, using a wooden spoon, stir it into the creamed butter and sugar. Mix until it is a stiffish dough. Sprinkle flour on a work surface, turn the dough on to it, and knead. Then using a floured rolling pin, roll out to a thickness of about $\frac{1}{4}$ in (6 mm). Cut into circles about 2 in (5 cm) in diameter and put them on to a greased baking sheet. Bake in a moderate oven, 350°F (180°C) Gas mark 4 (middle of the bottom right-hand oven of a 4-door Aga) for 10–12 minutes, until the biscuits are pale golden and crisp. Remove from the oven, sprinkle with a little caster sugar and leave for a minute on the baking sheet. Then gently lift them on to a cooling rack. When quite cold, store in an airtight tin.

Chocolate Oatmeal Crisp Biscuits

These chocolatey biscuits are similar to the vanilla biscuits but have an extra crunch provided by the oatmeal. These, too, seem to vanish as soon as they are made.

Makes about 18–20

---

4 oz (125 g) butter
3 oz (75 g) caster sugar
4 oz (125 g) plain flour
1 oz (25 g) cocoa

a few drops of vanilla
  essence
1 oz (25 g) medium oatmeal

Put the butter in a bowl and beat until smooth, then beat in the caster sugar, until well creamed. (This can be done in a food processor if you have one.) Sieve the flour and cocoa and stir into the creamed mixture with the vanilla essence and oatmeal, mixing thoroughly. You will have a stish dough.

Roll out on a floured work surface to a thickness of about $\frac{1}{4}$ in (6 mm), and cut into circles about 2 in (5 cm) in diameter. Put the circles on a greased baking sheet. Bake in a moderate oven, 350°F (180°C) Gas mark 4 (middle of the bottom right-hand oven of a 4-door Aga) for 10–12 minutes. Remove them from the oven and leave on the baking sheet for a minute, then carefully lift them on to a cooling rack. When they are quite cold store them in an airtight tin.

Spiced Orange Shortbread

A lightly spiced and orange-flavoured shortbread makes a nice change from a plain one. It is a delicious accompaniment to fruity puddings, even just plain stewed fruit.

Makes 12 pieces

---

6 oz (175 g) butter	1 rounded teaspoon ground
6 oz (175 g) plain flour	mixed spice
2 oz (50 g) semolina or	½ rounded teaspoon ground
ground rice	cinnamon
2 oz (50 g) caster sugar	caster sugar for dusting
finely grated rind of 1 orange	

Put all the ingredients together in a bowl and, using a knife, cut the butter into the dry ingredients, until the butter is in small pieces. Then, using your hands, rub the butter in until the mixture is like fine breadcrumbs. Knead it into a lump. Grease a baking tin about 6 by 8 in (15 by 20 cm) and press the shortbread dough into the tin as evenly as possible. Prick the shortbread all over, in rows, with a fork, and bake in a low to moderate oven, 325°F (170°C) Gas mark 3 (bottom of the bottom right-hand oven of a 4-door Aga) for 35–40 minutes, until the shortbread is biscuit-coloured but not browned. Remove from the oven, and dust immediately with caster sugar. Cool for 5–10 minutes, then cut into fingers about 1½ by 2½ in (4 by 6 cm). Lift the shortbread fingers out and cool them on a wire rack.

Almond Biscuits

Whilst these biscuits are delicious on their own at tea, I generally make them to accompany a fruit mousse, ice cream or sorbet. They keep well in an airtight container.

Makes about 18 biscuits

---

4 oz (125 g) plain flour
2 oz (50 g) ground almonds
2 oz (50 g) icing sugar,
   sieved
4 oz (125 g) butter

½ teaspoon almond essence,
   optional
9 halved almonds

Sieve the flour and ground almonds together, then add the icing sugar. Cut the butter into the dry ingredients, add the almond essence and work it to a crumb-like consistency with the finger tips; then knead into a dough.

Break off bits about the size of a walnut and roll into balls between the palms of your hands. Put them on a lightly-greased baking sheet, and flatten each ball. Press a halved (or flaked) almond into the middle of each. Bake in a low to moderate oven, 325°F (170°C) Gas mark 3 (bottom of the bottom right-hand oven of a 4-door Aga) until golden brown, about 15–20 minutes. Cool for a couple of minutes on the baking sheet, then gently lift them on to a cooling rack.

Raisin & Walnut Slices

The brandy in this recipe is not essential, you can substitute fresh orange juice, but the brandy does give a definite kick. Our children love it . . .

Makes about 16

---

4 oz (125 g) butter
4 oz (125 g) caster sugar
3 large eggs
6 oz (175 g) plain flour
1 rounded teaspoon baking powder
4 fl oz (125 ml) brandy or fresh orange juice

8 oz (225 g) raisins
4 oz (125 g) chopped walnuts
2 oz (50 g) mixed peel, or leave out the peel and increase the raisins by 2 oz (50 g)
caster sugar for dusting

Grease a baking tin about 8 by 10 in (20 by 25 cm) and line with siliconised paper. Put the butter in a bowl and beat it, adding the caster sugar bit by bit. Beat together thoroughly until light and creamy. Beat in the eggs, one by one, beating really well between each one. Sieve together the flour and baking powder, and stir them into the butter and egg mixture; stir in the brandy, raisins, walnuts and mixed peel.

Put the mixture into the prepared baking tin, smoothing it down evenly, and bake in a moderate oven, 350°F (180°C) Gas mark 4 (middle of the bottom right-hand oven of a 4-door Aga) for 25–30 minutes or until when you stick a knife in it comes out clean. Remove from the oven and leave in the tin for a couple of minutes. Dust a little caster sugar over the surface and cut into fingers about 2 by 3 in (5 by 7.5 cm). Cool in the tin, then lift out carefully and store in an airtight container.

Iced Lemon Curd & Coconut Squares

These make a delicious change from the chocolatey things which tend to feature on our tea-tables. They don't take long to put together, and spreading the lemon curd on the cake while the latter is still warm makes the curd melt into the cake.

Makes about 16

---

4 oz (125 g) butter
4 oz (125 g) caster sugar
2 large eggs
4 oz (125 g) self-raising
    flour
1 lb (450 g) lemon curd

4 oz (125 g) sieved icing
    sugar
fresh lemon juice
3 rounded tablespoons
    desiccated coconut

Grease a baking tin about 8 by 10 in (20 by 25 cm) and line it with siliconised paper. Put the butter in a bowl (you can do the whole thing in a food processor if you have one) and beat it, adding the caster sugar bit by bit. Beat until the mixture is pale in colour and well creamed. Beat in the eggs, one at a time, beating well between each one. Sieve the flour and stir it in. Pour and scrape this mixture into the prepared tin, and bake in a moderate oven, 350°F (180°C) Gas mark 4 (middle of the bottom right-hand oven of a 4-door Aga) for 20–25 minutes, or until when you push a knife or skewer into the cake it comes out clean. Remove the tin from the oven, and immediately spread the lemon curd all over the cake. Lift the cake out of the tin on its paper and leave to cool on a wire rack. Mix the icing sugar to the consistency of thick cream with lemon juice, and spread it over the cooled cake. Sprinkle the coconut evenly over the top. Cut into squares, and store in an airtight tin.

Sweet Sauces

S auces can often add the finishing touch to a pudding. Every sauce in this chapter is extremely easy to make, and some keep quite well and so can conveniently be made ahead.

Brandy & Orange Butter

This heavenly butter is for eating with Christmas pudding, or other steamed puds, and mince pies.

---

4 oz (125 g) butter	*4 tablespoons brandy*
4 oz (125 g) soft brown sugar	*grated rind of 2 oranges*

Put the butter in a bowl and, using a hand-held electric whisk, beat until creamy. Gradually beat in the brown sugar, then the brandy, beating as you add it spoonful by spoonful to the butter mixture. Lastly, beat in the grated orange rind. Pack into a small bowl and cover. This keeps for several weeks in the fridge.

Chocolate Sauce

This sauce keeps well in a covered container in the fridge. When cold it gets very thick, so warm the container slightly to help you spoon it into a saucepan to reheat for serving. It is the best chocolate sauce I have ever come across – thick yet runny and extremely dark and chocolatey.

Serves 5–6

---

6 oz (175 g) sugar	*3 tablespoons golden syrup –*
1 teaspoon vanilla essence	*dip the spoon into very hot*
3 level tablespoons cocoa	*water before you take each*
3 oz (75 g) butter	*spoonful of syrup, that*
¼ pint (150 ml) water	*way the syrup slips easily*
	off the spoon, and you get
	a true measure

Put all the ingredients together in a saucepan, and put the pan on a moderate heat. Stir until the butter is melted and the sugar dissolved, then boil for 3–5 minutes. The longer you boil it, the fudgier the sauce becomes. Serve warm, over a multitude of puddings, but perhaps best of all with ice cream and frozen puddings.

Fudge Sauce

This sauce rivals the chocolate sauce both in popularity and in ease of making. It is not for consumption by those on a cholesterol-conscious diet, but it is so good that it is well worth slimmers falling off their wagon of austerity and having a binge on a pudding with fudge sauce!

Serves 6

¼ pint (150 ml) double
   cream
4 oz (125 g) butter

4 oz (125 g) soft brown
   sugar

Put all the ingredients into a saucepan over a gentle heat, and stir as the butter melts and the sugar dissolves. Then boil fast for 5 minutes, and keep warm until you are ready to serve it. If (unlikely!) you should have any left over, it keeps perfectly well in the fridge for several days. Serve with vanilla ice cream or poached pears.

Rhubarb & Ginger Sauce

If you have any of this sauce left over, it freezes well.

Serves 6

---

2 lb (900 g) rhubarb cut in
  chunks about 1 in
  (2.5 cm) long
about 4 oz (125 g) sugar

2 rounded teaspoons ground
  ginger
6 pieces of ginger preserved
  in syrup, drained,
  optional

Put the chunks of rhubarb into a saucepan, together with
the sugar and ground ginger, and put a lid on. Put the pan
on a gentle to moderate heat; as it heats, the juice will seep
from the rhubarb, and this makes for a much better end
result rather than starting the rhubarb off with water. As
the juice flows, turn up the heat a bit, and cook until the
rhubarb is starting to fall apart – about 30 minutes.
Remove the saucepan from the heat and cool. Liquidise in
a blender, then sieve the purée. This may sound unnecessary (I loathe washing sieves), but it is worth it to get
an absolutely velvety sauce. Taste, and add more sugar if
you like, and a bit more ginger, if you think it needs it. If
you are using the preserved ginger, cut it into little slivers
and stir them through the sauce.

Vanilla Cream Sauce

Vanilla being one of my favourite flavours, this is one of my favourite sauces. It is the sauce I always make to serve, along with Brandy and Orange Butter, with Christmas pud, and it enhances any hot pudding. It isn't exactly essential to make it at the last minute, but I leave it to be the final item to do before any guests arrive. If it sits for too long, you tend to get a slightly watery separation at the bottom of the serving bowl. Don't let this put you off – it is a sauce I could eat by itself, spoonful by spoonful, so delicious is it.

Serves 6–8

---

3 eggs	*¼ pint (150 ml) double*
2 rounded tablespoons caster	*cream, lightly whipped*
sugar	*1 teaspoon vanilla essence*

Put the eggs and caster sugar in a bowl over a saucepan of gently simmering water, and whisk until pale and very thick. Remove the bowl from the saucepan, and continue whisking the mixture for about 5 minutes as it cools. The longer you whisk it as it cools, the less likelihood of separation. Leave to cool completely.

When it is quite cold, fold in the whipped cream and vanilla essence, and pour into a sauce-boat or serving bowl.

Mincemeat & Brandy (or Rum) Sauce

This sauce is guaranteed to warm you through on a cold winter's day. It is good with vanilla ice cream, and even better if made with home-made Mincemeat (page 122). This sauce is so easy to make it almost embarrasses me to write it out – but for that same reason I hope you will appreciate it as I do! Any left over can be stored in a jar.

Serves 6

---

1 lb (450 g) mincemeat
4 tablespoons brandy, or rum

grated rind of 1 orange

Put all the ingredients together in a saucepan and heat gently. Try not to let it simmer, because then the alcohol will evaporate! Serve hot, with home-made vanilla ice cream.

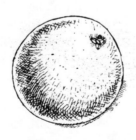

Cherry Jam & Brandy

Like the mincemeat sauce, this sauce is embarras[singly]
easy to make. But it is delicious, and much enjoyed by a[ll]
who eat it. I serve it with plain home-made vanilla ice
cream. If you use cherry brandy, you get a sweeter sauce
than if you use plain brandy. Any left over can be stored in
a covered jar. Sometimes I double the brandy for an extra
boozey sauce.

Serves 6

1 lb (450 g) cherry jam	*4 tablespoons either cherry brandy or plain brandy*

Put the two ingredients together in a saucepan and warm
through gently, until the jam melts. Try not to let the sauce
boil, as then the alcohol will evaporate. Serve the sauce
hot, with good vanilla ice cream.

...raspberries when they've been
...magine the wonderful smell of
...g, you will know the flavour I'm
...his sauce is jewel-like in colour, and
...nnamon, a spice which enhances the
...of raspberries. It is delicious served with
...Meringues (page 92). It is also good with
va... ...eam. As with any sauce, it adds the final touch
to a d... ...oth in appearance and taste.

Serves 6

1½ lb (700 g) raspberries
1 rounded dessertspoon
  ground cinnamon

3 rounded tablespoons caster
  sugar

Put the raspberries into a saucepan, together with the
caster sugar and cinnamon, and put the pan on a gentle to
moderate heat, until the juices begin to run from the
raspberries. Heat until the raspberries begin to fall apart,
and the sugar dissolves, then remove the saucepan from the
heat, and cool. Liquidise in a blender, and sieve the sauce
because the little pips in the raspberries never break down
in the blender. Serve cold, in a sauceboat or bowl, with the
vanilla meringues piled on a separate plate or ashet.

Index

Lime:
 Fresh lime pie, 48–9
 Fresh lime soufflé, 70–71
 Fresh lime water ice, 32

M
Marzipan:
 Cointreau and chocolate
  marzipan balls, 128
Meringue: 52, 61, 80–92
 Apple and mincemeat
  meringue pie, 52–3
 Chocolate meringues with
  brandy flavoured cream,
  83–4
 Crunchy almond meringue
  cake, 87–8
 Crunchy brown sugar
  meringues with rhubarb and
  ginger sauce, 84–5
 Gâteau Diane, 86–7
 Ginger meringue bombe, 91
 Ginger meringues with orange
  and ginger cream, 82
 Orange meringue bombe with
  hot chocolate sauce, 90–91
 Pavlova, 85–6
 Pineapple meringue pudding,
  61–2
 Strawberry cream meringue
  cake with coffee icing, 89–90
 Vanilla meringues with
  raspberry and cinnamon
  sauce, 92
Mincemeat: 122
 Apple and mincemeat
  meringue pie, 52–3
 Baked appled stuffed with
  mincemeat, with orange
  sabayon sauce, 62–3
 Mincemeat and brandy (or
  rum) sauce, 160
Mint:
 Apricot and mint jam, 116–17

Mint (*cont.*)
 Iced blackcurrant and mint
  parfait, 20–21
 Mint jelly, 115–16
 Vanilla and chocolate mint
  crisp ice cream, 28–9
Mousses: 66–77
 Apricot and orange mousse,
  76–7
 Crushed raspberry mousse,
  71–2
 Fresh lime soufflé, 70–71
 Kirsch and black cherry
  mousse, 74–5
 Rhubarb and ginger mousse,
  72–3
 Strawberry and orange
  mousse, 75–6
Mulled wine and black grape
  jelly, 69–70
Mustard, home-made, 119

N
Nesselrode ice cream, 23–4

O
Orange:
 Apricot and orange mousse,
  76–7
 Baked apples stuffed with
  mincemeat, with orange
  sabayon sauce, 62–3
 Brandy and orange butter, 156
 Fresh orange jelly, 68
 Ginger meringues with orange
  and ginger cream, 82
 Iced orange cream, 22–3
 Orange marmalade, 114–15
 Orange meringue bombe with
  hot chocolate sauce, 90–91
 Spiced orange shortbread, 151
 Strawberry and orange
  mousse, 75–6

Notes

Notes

Notes

CELEBRATIONS
by Claire Macdonald of Macdonald

Celebrations is written for anyone who likes to eat and drink well, and to celebrate the milestones in their lives. Almost any event can be an excuse for a party or a feast – birthdays, Christmas, anniversaries, christenings or even just a summer party or barbecue – and Claire Macdonald, who runs a family hotel at Kinloch Lodge on the Isle of Skye, offers a host of delicious recipes to help even the most hard-pressed cook to celebrate life.

Menus range from romantic dinners for two to lunch or dinner parties for twenty or more. *Celebrations* also includes a stunning selection of the puddings for which Claire Macdonald is so justly famous.

Above all, the recipes are supremely practical and many can be prepared in advance; *Celebrations* is aimed at those of us who love to entertain but have to cope with busy lives as well.

'Claire Macdonald of Macdonald is plainly one of nature's hostesses . . . the recipes are many of them novel as well as practical'
Glasgow Herald

0 552 99436 7

LUNCHES
by Claire Macdonald of Macdonald

'Umpteen mouthwatering ideas from the simple to the grand'
Sunday Post

Lunch is a word which can be interpreted in many different ways: a robust Sunday roast with all the traditional accompaniments, or a more informal meal of soup or pasta. But most people recognize lunch, particularly at the weekend, as a time to get together, to catch up on news, to entertain, and above all to enjoy good food.

Claire Macdonald's *Lunches* is a wonderful collection of recipes which will suit every kind of midday meal. From recipes for business lunches, like savoury profiteroles and goat's cheese roulade, to picnic and packed lunches such as game pasties, Scotch quails' eggs or sausage hotpot, Claire Macdonald has gathered together a truly mouthwatering array. She gives a chapter on brunch, including favourites like kedgeree, eggs benedict or muffins, as well as the more unusual pigs in blankets, and a selection of starters and main courses for special occasion lunches. Also provided are invaluable ideas for children's lunches, like home-made hamburgers, toad in the hole, or fishcakes. And Claire Macdonald's irresistible selection of puddings will ensure that the finest lunch is finished off to perfection.

'Claire Macdonald's recipes have just the right amount of enthusiasm and practicality'
The Examiner

0 552 14428 2

THE CLAIRE MACDONALD COOKBOOK
by Claire Macdonald of Macdonald

Clarissa Dickson Wright, now famous for her role in *Two Fat Ladies*, has described Kinloch Lodge on the Isle of Skye as 'the hotel where Claire Macdonald and her husband Godfrey cheerfully dispense peace, good humour and wonderful food'. Distilled from Claire's years of cooking at Kinloch Lodge, this is a celebratory collection of the best of the recipes from her many books together with much new material.

Revised and updated to take account of the health- and weight-conscious Nineties, the recipes range exhaustively across soups, first courses, fish, poultry and game, meat, eggs, vegetables (both as a main course and a side dish), salads, pasta and rice, stocks, sauces and a selection of delicious breads, cakes and puddings in every shape and form.

Claire Macdonald, whose hallmarks are the use of seasonal, fresh country ingredients, and practical, down-to-earth methods, is justly renowned for her cookery writing. Whether providing ideas for informal family fare, intimate gourmet meals or special occasion dishes, Claire is a remarkably reliable source of foolproof and marvellous recipes. *The Claire Macdonald Cookbook* is an indispensable addition to every cook's *batterie de cuisine*.

0 593 04268 9

NOW AVAILABLE AS A BANTAM PRESS HARDBACK

OTHER CLAIRE MACDONALD COOKERY TITLES AVAILABLE FROM CORGI BOOKS AND BANTAM PRESS

THE PRICES SHOWN BELOW WERE CORRECT AT THE TIME OF GOING TO PRESS. HOWEVER TRANSWORLD PUBLISHERS RESERVE THE RIGHT TO SHOW NEW RETAIL PRICES ON COVERS WHICH MAY DIFFER FROM THOSE PREVIOUSLY ADVERTISED IN THE TEXT OR ELSEWHERE.

□	99216 x	**SEASONAL COOKING**	£6.99
□	99288 7	**MORE SEASONAL COOKING**	£6.99
□	99436 7	**CELEBRATIONS**	£7.99
□	14209 3	**SUPPERS**	£6.99
□	14428 2	**LUNCHES**	£6.99
□	04268 9	**THE CLAIRE MACDONALD COOKBOOK** (Hardback)	£25.00

All Transworld titles are available by post from:

Bookpost, P.O. Box 29, Douglas, Isle of Man IM99 1BQ

Credit cards accepted. Please telephone 01624 836000, fax 01624 837033, Internet http://www.bookpost.co.uk or e-mail: bookshop@enterprise.net for details.

Free postage and packing in the UK. Overseas customers allow £1 per book (paperbacks) and £3 per book (hardbacks).